Robert Hardy

THE WITCHES' HEXAGRAM

A Wiccan View of the Cabbala

B°A BIBLIOTHECA
LEXANDRINA

Published as *The Witches' Hexagram*
by Bibliotheca Alexandrina Ltd 2019
www.bibliotheca-alexandrina.co.uk
Lydney 2019

ISBN 978-0-993910-5-7

Cover and layout design by Agnieszka Hulewicz
Photo on the cover by JR Korpa on Unsplash

Contents

Acknowledgments

I would like to say a special thanks to Gerry Greenslade for setting my feet on the path. Thanks also to my wife Jan for all her help with the pathworkings.

Foreword

Remember the American TV series Bewitched, which was aired on British television in the sixties? Bewitched had a huge influence on the young Robert Hardy. I just didn't admire Samantha – I wanted to be her, to be a witch!

My desire to become a witch did not wane, and as I aged it led me to read books on magic and witchcraft by such luminaries as Doreen Valiente, Patricia Crowther, Gerald Gardner, Dr Margaret Murray, and others.

I sent out several letters to the Witches Mill and other likely addresses. I don't know if any of my letters reached their intended goals, but I received no replies, so my search for a coven fell on stony ground.

By this time Angie, my first wife, and I had set up home together in a flat above a cobbler's shop in Dursley. What drew us together was our shared interest in the Craft. Peter was one of the small group of friends we hung out with in the late sixties. One day, he placed a student newsletter from Bristol University in my hand. He gave me an awkward smile, then opened the pamphlet to the back pages and placed his finger on a small ad. I can't remember the exact wording, but the gist of it was: "If you are interested in joining a witch coven, ring this number."

That very evening, I stood in my local phone box, coins in hand. The number was written on the back of a cigarette box (we all smoked back then.)

I carefully dialled the number, my heart racing as I listened to the ring tones at the other end. "Hello," came a soft voice. I gingerly explained about the ad and my fervent desire to become a witch.

After a brief exchange of names and details, about where we lived and ages etc. we decided to meet up in Bristol the following weekend.

I was told that the address of the meeting place would be kept secret for the time being, in case we were journalists or something along those lines. I explained we didn't own a car. That was not a problem: if we could arrive around midday someone would pick us up at the bus station. I was to ring back and tell them what time my bus would arrive. This I did, and we agreed that we would be picked up outside Bristol central bus station by a man called Charles, driving a black Rover limousine.

Saturday lunchtime we walked out from Bristol bus station and waited outside on the cold pavement. It was a grey day, but luckily dry. Standing there all expectant, we didn't have to wait long until a smartly dressed older man approached us and asked us, "Robert and Angie?" "Yes," we answered. Charles shook my hand, kissed Angie on the cheek, and introduced himself. Together we walked a little way up the street to where Charles' black Rover was parked. He opened the back door and invited us to climb in.

To keep our intended destination secret, we were offered blindfolds. Whether it was the will of the Gods or our youthful optimism, we sat back and resigned ourselves to our fate.

After many stops and starts as the limousine drove around the City streets of Bristol, we pulled up to the sound of the handbrake being applied and I knew we had reached our destination. Charles switched off the engine. Still wearing the blindfolds, we were helped up a set of stone steps leading to the front door. I expect our arrival was observed through the downstairs windows, because the front door opened immediately. I was ushered in to the murmur of voices, Angie close behind me, followed by the sound of the front door closing. The first thing that struck me was the smell of high grade church incense mingled with the strong odour of cats!

I was led through the building to a back room. Once inside, I was told to stand. The atmosphere in the room was electric, and after a minute or two someone removed my blindfold. The room was lit by candlelight. Several people, both men and women, stood around me, each barefooted and robed, masks covering their faces (adepts of the coven, I rightly assumed).

What was before me took my breath away. A figure wearing a goat head mask and black ceremonial robes sat behind a table draped in black cloth. Two black candles flanked the strange figure. Smoke from a large brass thurible rose up and weaved its way around the horns.

"I have arrived home!" I thought.

Someone placed a stool for me to sit on. Then, the goat-headed priest asked me why I thought I deserved initiation into the Craft. I can't remember my answer, but they seemed pleased with it, and the interview was over. A woman with long blond hair wearing a cat mask knelt down before me and offered me a drink of red wine from a silver chalice, then bade me welcome.

The goat-headed priest removed his mask and gave me a wicked simile. That man was Gerry Greenslade, High Priest of the coven, and the girl in the cat mask its High Priestess.

Next, it was Angie's turn. I was led out of the room as she was led in. Head high and still wearing her blindfold, she vanished into the smoky temple. Later, she described her experiences and interview to me. That's Angie's story, and not mine to tell.

In the months that followed after that fateful day, we travelled the road to Bristol many times learning our magical trade. Gerry in later years said we took to witchcraft like a pair of ducks to water.

And that, my friend, is how I got into the craft. I owe Gerry Greenslade a great gift of gratitude for teaching me about life, the Cabbala and all manner of magical disciplines. Gerry himself was initiated in London in 1969 by Alex Sanders and Maxine, and after founding the Bristol coven in Miner Road, Gerry kept in close contact with both of them.

Introduction

Following on from my book *The Witches' Pyramid, The Witches' Hexagram* is the second book in the series. It explores the middle of the Cabalistic Tree of Life. Working through the first book should arm you with the necessary knowledge to start working through *The Witches' Hexagram.*

The Witches' Hexagram covers the centre of the Tree of Life which reveals the character of the three Sephiroth, Geburah, Chesed, and Tiphareth, and the eight central paths linking them with each other and with the lower Sephiroth. Over the course of this book you will become familiar with them and all the treasures they hold.

The central hexagram also covers the seven classical planets. Since the hexagram has six points, the seventh planet, the Sun, sits in the centre of it, and is assigned to the Sephira Tiphareth.

The remaining orbiting six planets help model the flavour of the Sephiroth in which they reside.

Like *The Witches' Pyramid, The Witches' Hexagram* is self-contained. In this book you will work mainly within its boundaries, and hopefully you won't wander outside its remit.

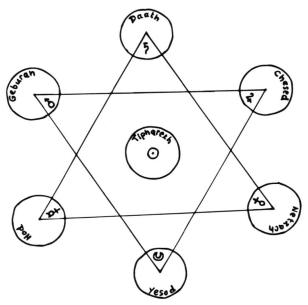

Hexagram in the centre of Tree of Life.

As you can see, the Hexagram is made up of two equilateral tri-angles, one placed over the other. The hexagram brings the two conflicting triangles together into one symbol.

These two triangles represent several things, the most common interpretations being: Fire and Water, Man and Woman, Eve and Adam Kadmon, and the Macrocosmic and Microcosmic principles of "As above, so below."

The conflicting qualities of the two triangles are kept in har-mony by bringing them together in the symbol of the hexagram and placing the authority of the Sun in the centre, in which sits Tiphareth, the Sephira of balance and harmony.

The uppermost point of the hexagram rests in Daath, which loosely represents the planet Saturn. Daath is that mysterious sphere located on the 13th path, Tiphareth to Kether. The path's tarot card is The High Priestess, the queen of hidden mysteries, the very essence of the word 'occult'.

Daath is one of mysteries of the Tree of Life. It is written that the Tree of Life has ten Sephiroth: not nine, not eleven, but ten! And yet most Cabbalists and magicians accept that it exists. Its working energy is said to be formed from the knowledge and wisdom of the magician who travels the paths on the Tree of Life, so if you accept this theory, the more magical work you do, the grander Daath will appear.

I met a man upon the stair, and when I looked he wasn't there. He wasn't there again today, oh, how I wish he'd go away. That's Daath in a nutshell!

As I have mentioned, Daath has the planet Saturn assigned to it. Saturn, the Roman God after whom the planet is named, the dark mysterious lord of time and agriculture is sober in character. If Daath is an illusionary sphere, Saturn's position in Daath is also phantasmal and wraith-like.

The planet's true position on the Tree of Life is firmly established in the Sephira Binah, the Great Mother.

Interestingly, the hexagram has a link with an early witchcraft mark called the daisy wheel hex mark.

These hex marks can be found carved onto stone walls and wooden panels inside churches, farmhouses, cottages, and other places. In houses, they are most commonly found around thresholds and fireplaces. These are not marks left by builders, carpenters, or masons. Those workmen marks are all well catalogued.

The hex marks are genuine magical talismans. The daisy wheel marks are clearly marked out with the aid of the pair of compasses. The most common have six petals, hence the name hex marks, as in "to put a hex on someone."

These hex marks began to appear from 1606 onwards, during reign of King James I. He was famous for his King James Bible and infamous for his fanatical stance on Witchcraft. Were hex marks placed there to protect the King from the witches, or to protect the witches from the King? (This information was gleaned from the book: *The British Book of Spells and Charms* by Graham King, past curator of the Museum of Witchcraft, Boscastle, Cornwall).

I have included this information is because it's interesting to see how past witchcraft practices match the more recent Western Tradition. The daisy marks could represent the Sun rays, or even with a stretch of the imagination, the seven classic planets with the Sun at its centre. (The classic planets are those visible with the naked eye.)

Daisy wheel hex marks.

Introduction

Like my first book, *The Witches' Pyramid*, *The Witches' Hexagram* deals with the concept of the Path of the Serpent which crawls up the Tree of Life, taking in all ten Sephiroth and the 22 pathworkings on its way. The Path of the Serpent is the path of the magician and witch. Magical knowledge is power, and through this power comes enlightenment. Others find that delving into every dark corner and looking up the metaphysical chimney to see the stars is not their way. They prefer to stay with the middle pillar of devotion.

1. Meditations of balance and enlightenment

Cabalistic Cross

Before we start our pathworking, it is important to learn the Cabalistic Cross, a meditation technique used to balance your body and cleanse your aura.

The Cabalistic Cross is a shortened version of the Adam/Eve Kadmon exercise, which is given in full at the end of this chapter. Nevertheless, being shorter in no way diminishes its value as a tool to help you prepare for Cabalistic ritual or pathworking.

Performing the Cabalistic Cross should become second nature to you. It is a ritual after all, and all ritual is a prerequisite to any given act or performance. Once it becomes habit, it starts to work on a subliminal level.

Having said that, it is vital to speak the words out loud so your breath gives them life. Similarly, visualise the colours spinning at their allotted places on your body. This will reinforce your connection with the Sephiroth. Familiarity can lead to complacence, just going through the actions, so be aware, concentrate, and strive to be perfect.

Although the Cabalistic Cross falls into the category of hermetics, sound (voice), arm gestures, and other stimuli such as the use of incense and the like reinforce its effect on you and the universe about you.

Stand up and face East. Set your feet firmly on the ground, shake out your arms and hands, rotate your head, and relax. Breathe slowly and deeply.

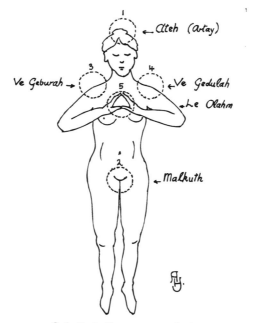

Cabalistic Cross on your body.

Cross your hands over your chest and empty your mind. When you are ready, place the forefingers and thumbs together to from an upwards pointing triangle. Raise your hands, still holding the triangle gesture, and place your triangle of manifestation over your forehead, point up. Visualise brilliant white light radiating from your hands to ignite and join with the spinning disc of Kether and vibrate the word 'Ateh'.

Next, lower your hands over your genital area, flipping your hands so that now the triangle points down, and vibrate the word Malkuth. Feel the power rushing up from the ground and forming the spinning disc of Malkuth with all its brilliant golden autumn colours.

Next, raise your hands to cover your right shoulder, pointing up, and vibrate the words: 'Ve-Geburah'. Visualise a spinning disc of ruby red light.

Cross your upper chest and place your hands over your left shoulder, points up, and vibrate the word: 'Ve-Gedulah', and visualise a spinning disc of sapphire blue light.

Finally, place your hands over your heart centre and intone: 'Le--Olam', visualising a spinning disc of golden light.

The Cabalistic Cross is one piece of Cabalah that witches will be familiar with, because it is part of the Book of Shadows.

In my book, *The Witches' Pyramid*, I cover the background and the meaning of the Cabalistic Cross in some depth.

Needless to say, the ritual and gestures performed in the act of invoking the Cabalistic Cross turn the Tree of Life and your body, mind, and spirit into one entity. In *The Witches' Pyramid* I venture to explain the similarity between the Cabalistic Cross and the Christian cross.

A common mistake is to be confused by the difference between the plain Christian cross and the Calvary cross. The Calvary cross depicts the crucifixion of Jesus Christ. The plain cross does not! The unadorned cross is an early hieroglyph of man. The T-shaped cross or Tau cross is a simpler form, though in religious iconography it is perhaps earlier still, but that is open to debate.

The Hebrew letter Tau (meaning cross) is situated on the 32nd path, Malkuth to Yesod. The path's tarot card is The Universe or The World, depending on which pack you use. The number value of the Hebrew letter Tau is 400.

Number crunching time!

The Cabalistic Tree of Life is made up of ten basic Sephiroth (spheres). Each individual Sephira has its own microcosmic Tree of Life hidden within it. So, ten times ten gives you a theoretical one hundred Sephiroth.

As we know, the Tree of Life can be separated into four, to represent the formula of tetragrammaton or the four lettered word: Yod Heh Vau Heh:

- Fire (Father)
- Water (Mother)
- Air (Son)
- Earth (Daughter).

Yod, Heh, Vau, Heh as the image of the divine being.

Add these four worlds of the Cabalah to the equation, and you have a possible 400 wonderful Sephiroth. This way Tau represents the universe, 400 wonderful things!

Having a Tree of Life inside each Sephira: how does that work?

For a reasonable example we need something that is contained, and has a definite purpose and genre.

What about a theatre? The London Palladium for instance would make a perfect example. The theatre is far more then bricks and mortar: its purpose is to entertain and amaze. All life is contained within its walls, its toilets, its bars, all the staff that make a living there, the audience that laugh and cry, the raw emotion conjured up under the spotlights. The essential point being, that with all its life and conflicts it is basically The London Palladium.

Each Sephira is similar to a theatre. Take Netzach for instance. All the energies of the other nine Sephiroth flow into its heart. All the myths and magic, both astrological and mythological, are in Netzach, filling its own special depths, but with all its complex structure and mystery. Its temple stands proudly on its rosy mount and acclaims: "I AM NETZACH."

There are other connections with the Cabalistic Cross that I would like to explore, such as the way both Catholic and Anglican branches of the Church use the three touch blessing with the words: "The Father, Son, and Holy Ghost."

The Pope and his priests use this simple gesture when they stand before their congregation. In the case of the Pope addressing the crowds in the Vatican, his benediction is expected and loved.

A similar use for this three-touch blessing is found across Europe and beyond, and is used by less educated citizens to advert the evil eye.

Gerald Gardner, the father of modern Wicca, and Cecil Williamson, founder of the Witchcraft Museum on the Isle of Man, which is now situated in the charming fishing village of Boscastle in Cornwall, both reported proudly that on occasion locals would cross themselves, then cross to the other side of the street to avert the evil eye when either of these gentlemen approached.

Adam and Eve Kadmon exercise

The Adam and Eve exercise is a method of opening up all ten Sephiroth on your body. Along with the illustration of Adam/Eve Kadmon, I have written a description of where all ten Sephiroth are stationed on your body.

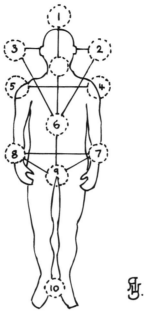

Adam/Eve Kadmon

The Path of the Serpent starts at Malkuth, the tenth Sephira, its four colours being olive, citrine, russet, and black, traditionally associated with the Queen scale.

There are four different colour scales associated with the Tree of Life. The King scale, the Queen scale, the Knight scale, and the Princess scale. All colours used in the course of this book are in the Queen scale or the Angelic scale, also referred to as the Briah scale.

From Malkuth, the serpent winds its way up the Tree of Life, touching each individual Sephira and path on its way, finally reaching its goal in Kether the Crown.

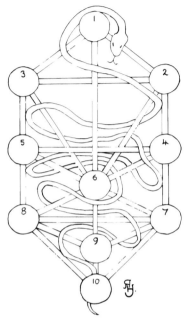

Path of the Serpent

Just like the serpent moves, we will invoke Adam/Eve Kadmon starting at the feet and working our way up to the top of your head.

In all our pathworking we always start at Malkuth.

Malkuth sits at the bottom of the middle pillar of Mildness.

Malkuth is basically the ground beneath our feet. If you are wearing shoes and socks, take them off, so that you can feel the ground under you. It's like plugging yourself in.

Malkuth is visualised as a quartered disc made up of autumnal colours, traditionally olive, citrine, russet, and black, that you are standing on.

Malkuth is embodied by your feet and lower legs. The goat--legged Pan is emblematic of the fertile Earth.

Yesod is a different matter, sitting on the middle pillar of Mildness. Distinctly sensual in character, Yesod rules the sexual zone, upper thighs, genitals, womb, and anus. This is the power house of your body. The violet spinning disc of Yesod is self-contained and does not extend out to the hips (Hod and Netzach.)

However, when you are sexually aroused, the Odic energy inside your Yesod centre will travel up the spine, lighting you up like a Christmas tree as it goes up. This form of sexual energy is also called the Kundalini phenomenon. Kundalini is a Sanskrit word for snake, and it rests coiled up at the base of your spine. When you invoke Yesod onto your body, the normally dormant Kundalini serpent starts to wake up!

As I pointed out in my book, *The Witches' Pyramid*: anything to do with sex and magic is very addictive. You have been warned.

The eighth Sephira, Hod, is situated on your right hip, and visualised as a spinning orange disc of light. This is the seat of intelligence and learning, and is placed on the right-hand side pillar of Severity.

The seventh Sephira, Netzach, is placed on your left hip, and visualised as an emerald green spinning disc of light. It is situated on the pillar of Mercy on the left side of the body of Adam/Eve Kadmon.

Once you have invoked Netzach onto your left hip, you will have formed your first triangle of manifestation (also called the Astral Triangle) into which you can fill the sacred crucible with Odic energy.

The sixth Sephira, Tiphareth, is placed just below your heart centre at your solar plexus, and visualised as a spinning golden light. Tiphareth is located on the pillar of Mildness. Once activated, it connects your higher self to your personality. Everyday concerns will disappear and in their place a feeling of spiritual calm. I know this sound a little like spiritual claptrap, but believe me, even a short period free from the cares of everyday life will leave you feeling cleansed and even a little healed inside.

Let us move on to the fifth Sephira, Geburah, which is placed firmly on your right shoulder and visualised as a spinning disc of ruby red light. It is found on the right-hand pillar of Severity. If you were an angel, this Geburic energy would empower your right wing (your right arm). If you're not an angel, don't worry. On the Cabalistic Tree of Life anything is possible, even obtaining your own set of wings.

The fourth Sephira, Chesed, also known as Gedulah, is located on your left shoulder and visualised as a spinning disc of blue light. It empowers your left wing. With the invocation of Gedulah the second triangle of manifestation (also called the Ethical Triangle) is complete.

Once this second crucible is full of Moon/Sun energy (I have named this energy electrum after the gold and silver alloy of the ancient Greeks), this bodily energy electrum will call to the macrocosmic Godhead!

The third Sephira, Binah, is found on your right temple. Visualised as a spinning disc of black light, Binah is the quintessential Mother Goddess in her function as womb of space, where galaxies are formed.

The second Sephira, Chokmah, is located on your left temple, and visualised as a disc of spinning grey/white light. Chokmah is the Supernal Father who impregnated Binah by way of stardust. Chokmah is associated with the Zodiac.

The first Sephira and the last to be invoked is the mighty Kether, the Crown, and like a royal crown it sits on the top of your head. Visualise it as a circle of flaming white Yods descending to alight on your brow, similar to a circle of candles on a birthday cake.

These ten Sephiroth, once in place on the body, will transform you into Adam/Eve Kadmon. Before you start the Adam/Eve Kadmon exercise, study the diagram. Create your ritual space; incense and flowers help set the atmosphere. Empty your mind and proceed.

The Adam/ Eve Kadmon meditation

Picture yourself standing on a round disc divided into four equal quarters. Each segment is scattered with colourful autumn leaves. This quartered disc will be your sphere of Malkuth. The colours of the leaves denote the colours of Malkuth. Citrine, Olive, Russet, and Black, these four colours are reflected in the hues of the autumn leaves.

The four winds: Eurus, Notus, Zephyrus, and Boreas, that represent each of the four cardinal points, spin around the disc of Malkuth, lifting the leaves and spinning them around your legs like a whirlwind. The power of Malkuth spirals around your legs until it touches your Yesodic zone, located at the base of your spine and genitalia area.

Visualise a violet light expanding into a spinning disc. Touch this spot with your mind, and be conscious of your own sexuality.

Now activate your Hod and Netzach centres located on your right and left hip. Visualise Hod first as a spinning disc of bright orange light. Next, move across to Netzach on the left hip and visualise a spinning disc of emerald green light.

You have now completed your first triangle of manifestation using Yesod, Hod, and Netzach. This primary crucible will now be filled with Odic energy.

Concentrate on your Yesodic zone, within which sleeps the serpent of the Kundalini.

Let your personal serpent that lies dormant at the bottom of your spin awake and slowly uncoil, filling the triangle with its vitality.

Feel your sexuality, become aroused, and let the first triangle fill with your Odic force.

When this is accomplished, you can go on to the next stage.

Once the triangle is full, the energy will try and move up your spine and central column. Let it do so. Feel it travel towards your Tipharetic centre located at your solar plexus. The Kundalini energy reaches up and touches your Tiphareth centre at your solar plexus, striking at its heart like a viper.

The golden light of Tiphareth blazes out, embracing and absorbing this current of Odic energy, growing and spinning with golden light.

Now visualise the spheres of Geburah and Chesed shinning ruby red on your right shoulder and bright blue on your left. This outlines your second triangle.

Allow it to fill with the golden light of Tiphareth. Feed it all the time from Yesod below. When the second triangle is full, direct the combined energy of the Sun and Moon (electrum dynamism) up through your neck to the centre of your forehead. Then invoke Binah on the right temple. Visualise it as a spinning disc of black light. Cross to the left temple and invoke the power of Chokmah. Visualise it as a spinning disc of grey-white light.

Bring up more power from below, feel it rising up from the Earth through your middle column to energise Binah and Chokmah, so they form a link horizontally across your brow in the shape of a cosmic ribbon (a figure eight set on its side), this ancient infinity symbol vibrating across the third eye.

Next imagine a spinning crown of brilliant white Yods descend on your head. You are now at one with the universe, a huge towering figure, with your feet on the ground and your head in the stars.

To end your Adam/Eve Kadmon meditation, visualise your crown of Yods ascending from your head up into heavens. Then absorb the rest of the Sephiroth deep into your body.

Concentrating on the disc of Malkuth at your feet, visualise the autumn leaves floating back to their allotted quarters under your feet. Then vibrate the word of power: 'Adonai ha-Aretz' (Lord of the Earth) and return to the mundane world.

To finish, have something to eat and drink. That will ground you nicely.

Elemental Breathing exercise

In this exercise, you harness the breath of life with the power of your mind to visualise and mould the breath and mind together in a living elemental form.

Over the decades, myself and my magical brothers and sisters of the craft (you know who you are: Blessed Be) have performed the elemental breathing exercise many times in various forms.

Performed in circle, temple, and on sacred Hermetic paths, clearly this process like many described in this book is an end product of years of magical exploration.

The elemental breathing exercise is relatively simple to do, but brings big benefits if performed properly. So how to perform this wonder of bodily alchemy? And why, and what is its purpose?

The purpose and main benefit of performing the elemental breathing exercise is to balance the elements of Fire, Air, Water, and Earth in your corporal and spiritual body. The why is to embrace the four elements on a personal level and to hold them inside in perfect balance, hopefully leading to a better understanding of what it is like to be one of the elemental beings, whether they be Sylphs of the airy realms, Salamanders of the sacred flame, Undines of the streams and rivers, or Gnomes of the gardens of the Earth.

The best way to approach the elemental breathing exercise is to first divide your body into four separate zones.

- Your feet and legs will be assigned to the element of Earth.
- Your stomach and groin area will be assigned to the element of Water.
- Your chest and arms will be assigned to the element of Air.
- And your neck and head will be assigned the element of Fire.

The clever bit is you fill each of these zones by breathing in your chosen element. Starting with the Earth element, breathe it in and, using the power of your mind, direct it to your legs and feet. As you probably noticed, we do not invoke the Earth energy up from the ground as in other self-balancing and self-empowering exercises, e.g. Adam/Eve Kadmon, Cabalistic Cross, Middle Pillar etc. With the Elemental Breathing exercise, we simply pluck the elements out of the air with the breath. The four elements are all part of the ocean of air we all move in. In the Elemental Breathing exercise, we treat the magical elements in the same way as we treat the physical air, breathing them into our body, then directing them to their allotted place on your body.

Actually, this is easier to do them it sounds. Past practice has taught us that the best way to breathe in the elements is to transform them into a set of images related to the given element.

Earth for example is solid and heavy, and trying to breathe in part of a newly ploughed field would be a triumph of the magician's visualisation skills. So, let's lighten it up, imagining the Earth element as a string of flowers and greenery constructed from electric charged light of delicate colours and hues. Once you have breathed them into your body, and directed them to your feet and legs, you can solidify them into a weightier earth element.

For the Water element perhaps visualise silver fish, flashing with coloured lights, swimming through crystal clear waters: don't be tempted to invoke lunar energy. This is strictly about elements in the simplest form.

It goes without saying that the element of Air is easy, but you can still charge it with a touch of fairy dust.

Lastly, Fire. Try and invoke the feel of spiritual fire that purifies without burning or harming you. You could imagine sparking Salamanders running through the flames if you've a mind for the dramatic.

Right! Let's give it a try. First, as always loosen yourself up, then take a few moments to calm your mind. If you are using incense, choose carefully which aroma you use, because you don't want to be coughing halfway through the exercise.

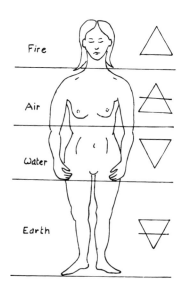

Four elements on woman's body

You can take as many breaths as needed to bring your chosen element inside your body and thus direct it to its allotted station, but to make the instructions uniform, I will use just four breaths in the text.

Once you are settled and prepared, deeply breathe in the element of Earth four times. Visualise the electric blue, green and red flowers chosen to represent your Earth energy. Inhale this energy of the Earth through your mouth, nose, and every pore in your skin. Let it fill you and direct it to your feet and legs. You will know when to move on to the next element, Water.

Repeat the exercise again, taking four deep breaths. This time, imagine crystal clear waters with their beautiful aquatic creatures swimming through them. Direct the element of Water into your stomach area.

When you are good and ready, breathe in the element of Air. The air is as fresh as breezes in far off mountain passes where the eagles beloved of Zeus stretch their wings. Fill your lungs and chest, and be free.

Lastly, with four breaths breathe in the element of Fire. Imagine it is a gift from the sacred temple lamps of the Sephiroth. Direct it up into your head like a beacon on the hill of coronation.

Now check yourself mentally. Feel your legs heavy with the power of the Earth. Next, imagine your stomach full of crystal clear Water, like your own inner lake washing and purifying your insides. Your chest is light and strong with the power of Air. Finally, let your divine flame consecrate and cleanse the mind, letting all negativity be consumed, leaving in its place only peace of mind.

Middle Pillar exercise

The Elemental Breathing exercise leads us nicely into the Middle Pillar exercise. This is a shortened version of the Adam/Eve Kadmon exercise. Instead of invoking all ten Sephiroth onto your body, you simply invoke the four Sephiroth that sit on the middle pillar of Mildness. These start from your feet up: Malkuth, Yesod,

Tiphareth, and Kether. This time, you will reinforce your connection with these four Sephiroth by intoning their respective divine names of power.

As always before you begin, relax your body and try to clear your mind from unnecessary chatter. Shake out your arms and stamp your feet: this will help to clear any unwanted stagnant energy, which may block your natural flow of energy. Take a few deep breaths, then starting at your feet visualise the quartered disc of Malkuth. Visualise the four colours: citrine, russet, olive, and black. The golds, reds, and greens of autumn leaves do it for me!

Once the image of the disc of Malkuth is firmly in your mind, energise it with its name of power: 'Adonai ha-Aretz'.

Now open the Yesodic centre located at your genital area. Focus your mind to see the spinning disc of violet light and invoke its power with the words: 'Shaddai El Chai'. Try to imagine the Moon shinning across a silver lake.

When this image as settled in your mind's eye, open up your golden heart centre Tiphareth and visualise a blazing golden yellow light. Now vibrate the name of power: 'Eloah ve Daath'.

Move the energy up into your head and invoke the crown of Kether with the words: 'Eheieh'.

Visualise a crown of shinning white Yods descending onto your brow. Try now to visualise all four Sephiroth blazing on your middle pillar. You should feel empowered and blessed all at the same time. You can stay in this state of grace for as long as you like. Usually, your body and mind will rebel after a while wishing to return to its earthy condition. Don't fight it, just slip out of your exercise, like slipping out of a magical robe. Then imagining the crown of Yods ascending up to heaven, letting the energy of Tiphareth and Yesod flow back down your middle pillar to earth once more in Malkuth.

2. The circle and the Sephiroth

The witches' circle and the Tree

Most practising witches place their altar in the northern quadrant of the circle in the belief that beyond the lands of ice and snow, and behind the north wind, is the land of the blessed dead, the land of the Hyperboreans.

It is said that the lights of aurora borealis are the souls of our ancestors dancing. Only the blessed dead can travel beyond their bounders.

There are other Wiccan mysteries associated with the North Star, and dance of Great and Little Bear that revolve around the North Star, also called the Spiral Castle.

Remember that one of the greatest modern benefactors, Santa Claus, is a god so powerful he doesn't even need to be believed in. And of course, he lives at the North Pole.

Not all covens opt to place their altar in the North. Some favour the Eastern quadrant, the station of the rising Sun, often referred to by magician as spiritual east. Christian Churches also place their altar in the East for similar reasons (light of the world etc.)

Whether you choose to position your altar in the North or East is a matter of personal choice.

Owning a small box that acts as an altar is invaluable, as you need somewhere to place certain artefacts, censer, chalice, pentacle, candles etc. Placing the altar close to the edge of the circle is more practical, freeing up the middle area for kneeling, blessing cakes and wine, and above all for romping!

Interestingly, in the Early Wiccan credo it states that the altar should be placed in the centre of the circle. Furthermore, it states that the High Priestess can be substituted for the altar, called the living altar. When doing so, the High Priestess positions herself so her yoni, the sacred chalice and the womb of life, is placed at the centre of the circle. This is played out to its final conclusion in the mysteries of the Third Degree.

This is where the witches' circle joins forces with the Cabalah. The tenth Sephira Malkuth houses the bride of the Microprosopus. She can be seen in one of her many forms in the centre of the tarot card The World.

As we know, the Cabalistic Tree of Life has four aspects to it, represented by the four elements, Fire, Water, Air, and Earth. So, in theory there are four Trees of life representing forty Sephiroth. If you imagine the four Trees of Life laid down flat inside your magic circle, they would form the profile of the equal armed cross also called the Solar Cross. The four Malkuths would then sit in the centre of your circle and mould into each other. This quartered disc will form the foundation of each of the four separate Trees.

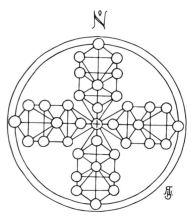

Magic circle with four Trees of Life

31

The four independent Kethers become the line of the circle's circumference, symbolising spirit and the male energy (Horned God). The four Trees each represent the physical world of the elements, symbolising female energy (Mother Goddess). Malkuth, the Kingdom, is now the point at the centre, the gateway though which all life flows. The Bride of the Microprosopus (the body of wisdom in the earthly realms) and the High Priestess have joined forces. So, the witches' circle is now fused with the whole Cabalistic Tree of Life. Its circle line, the spirit of your God, the four stations of North, East, South, and West plus their elements are the essence and grace of your holy Mother Goddess. You now have a representation of the whole known universe at your feet, as symbolised by the sacred magic circle.

In conclusion, if you're worried about where all this pathworking is leading you, don't fret! If the above assumption is correct, you won't even have left your own magic circle. Consequently, at all times you have been surrounded by the God and Goddess, in the embrace of Kether.

Whether this acceptance of Tree of Life fitting inside the circle is confined to the witch's credo, or is generally excepted as a sound magical theory, I am not sure. Having said that, I am fairly confident that all aspects of the magic circle have been intensely discussed at all levels and put into practice behind the closed doors of occultism; things to keep secret, my dears.

Gods and Goddess, and their place on the Tree of Life.

	Roman	Greek	Egyptian
Kether	Jupiter, sky father	Zeus, sky father	Nut, star goddess
Chokmah	Faunus	Pan	Amun
Binah	Juno	Hera	Isis
Chesed	Jupiter, city father	Poseidon	Osiris
Geburah	Mars	Ares	Horus
Tiphareth	Apollo	Apollo	Ra
Netzach	Venus	Aphrodite	Hathor
Hod	Mercury	Hermes	Thoth
Yesod	Diana	Artemis	Shu
Malkuth	Ceres	Persephone	Nephthys

3. The ten Sephiroth in descending order

Kether

Translation:	the Crown
Astrological:	Primum Mobile (First Mover)
Archangel:	Metatron
Order of angels:	Chaioth ha-Qadesh
	(Holy Living Creatures)
Colour on Queen scale:	white
Divine name:	Eheieh
Magical symbols:	the Crown, the mysterious Point,
	and the all-seeing eye

The first Sephira, Kether, is the ultimate imaginable by human consciousness. Beyond the Sephira Kether are the three bands of the unmanifest, or negative existence, which can also be likened to three planes or veils.

The first of these veils is called Ain, Negativity.

The second veil is called Ain Soph, the Limitless.

The final veil which is closest to Kether is called Ain Soph Aur, the Limitless Light. It is the outflowing of Ain Soph Aur that makes Kether become manifest.

These three veils are said to be by definition unknowable. In her book, The Cosmic Doctrine, Dion Fortune put forward a possible explanation for the three outer veils. She claimed that the clarification was given to her by one of the Masters (those initiates who chose to return to the Earthly plane to help others gain enlightenment.)

Dion Fortune's Master's Explanation

If you can imagine nothing, then envision nothing moving. This will form gravity and will pull the outer edge inward causing a circular motion. Nothing gyrating will attain a positive charge on its top and by virtue of balance, a negative charge on its bottom. The positive charge together with the negative charge will fight each other and cause friction, friction is energy which will change nothing into something and that something could be called Ain Soph Aur.

I Am that I Am!

Kether is the first manifestation, the prime mover, 'I am that I am', pure existence without form, and, until it gives rise to Chokmah, without obvious activity.

In theological terms, to attain the consciousness of Kether one needs to achieve fusion with the eternal.

Chokmah

Translation: Wisdom
Astrological: sphere of the zodiac
Archangel: Ratziel
Order of angels: Auphanim (Wheels)
Colour on Queen scale: grey (pearl-hued)
Divine name: Yah
Magical symbols: the phallus, the single line

Once Kether becomes active in Chokmah, the genie is truly out of the bottle. Called the Supernal Father, Chokmah is represented by the Hebrew letter Yod, the first letter in Tetragrammaton, the four lettered word. Yod, a drop of divine light, is also referred to as the cosmic sperm.

Chokmah is that pure rush of universal energy racing though the void of the unknown, unorganised leaping to and fro between its duel nature, like lighting in a bottle.

The magical image of Chokmah is a bearded male figure. If you're looking for God the Father, you have found him.

If you're looking for the horned God of the witches, look to a leaping Goat Foot God, reaching to the summit of all things! But don't panic.

Binah

Translation:	Understanding
Astrological:	planet Saturn
Archangel:	Tzaphkiel
Order of angels:	Aralim (Order of Thrones)
Colour on Queen scale:	black
Divine name:	Jehovah Elohim
Magical symbols:	the yoni, the triangle, and the chalice

The ecstatic force of Chokmah the all-begetting Father is gathered up and held in the womb of Binah, the great Mother. There, the stellar sperm will be organised into form. Having received boundless but undirected energy of Chokmah, Binah with set it to work creating form from force.

Binah the great Mother shares the vice of Malkuth: Inertia. This contradiction between creativity and the inertia is reflected in two names: Ama, the dark sterile Mother, and Aima, the bright fertile Mother.

This enigma could be seen in human terms, as summer and winter, or the womb resting during its menstrual cycle. Aima, by contrast represents the womb, fully ready to receive the sacred sperm and create life.

These two qualities are reflected by Binah being associated both with Juno and Saturn.

The Goddess Juno and her legend

Juno, also known by her Greek name Hera, means Splendour of Heaven, and according to others, just Lady.

Juno is sister and wife to Jupiter King of the Gods, thus giving her the esteemed title of Queen of the Gods.

Juno's original function was that of protectress and guardian to mortal women that prayed to her in times of distress. There is also a connection with the Moon, and at one time Juno was worshipped as a Moon Goddess.

Juno was the daughter of Cronus and Rhea, but was brought up by Oceanus and Tethys, in their dwelling away in the far west beyond the middle sea (Could this be the fabled land of Atlantis?)

Without prior knowledge of her parents, she was wedded to Jupiter in the garden of the Gods where ambrosial rivers flow. In celebration of the wedding the Earth sent up an unblemished tree, heavy with golden apples and coloured with the blush of the sunset. In some accounts it was referred to as the Tree of Life (the Biblical garden of Eden springs to mind).

Homer says: Juno was the worthy Goddess, a queenly, ox-eyed beauty. Hesiod said of Juno: Golden-sandalled and golden-throned, glrious beyond compare was her presence, when she harnessed her horses and drove forth into the world, in her golden wheeled chariot that Hebe made ready, that the Hours set aside!

Fearful too could be her wrath, for she is of a jealous disposition, and the vagaries of her husband Jupiter drove her at times to be vengeful, because Juno is proud as only a great goddess can be.

The cities that Juno favoured were Argos, Sparta, and Mycenae. The peacock and the cow are dear to her. Many sacred groves and wide pastures rejoiced in her name.

The mention that Hebe made ready Juno's chariot is interesting because Hebe is Juno's and Jupiter's daughter, goddess of youth and cup bearer to the Gods of Olympus. When her love for Hercules called, Hebe was replaced as cup bearer by a Trojan youth Ganymede, carried off from his haunts on the slopes of Mount Ida by Jupiter in his form of an Eagle.

Binah is the third and last Sephira on the Supernal Triangle ('Supernal' meaning "Entities in or belonging to the heaven of divine beings; celestial or divine".) Binah is the mother of restriction and movement and along with Cronus (Saturn) gives birth to the concept of time.

Chesed

Translation:	Mercy
Astrological:	planet Jupiter
Archangel:	Tzadkiel
Order of angels:	Chashmalim (Brilliant Ones)
Colour on Queen scale:	blue
Divine name:	El
Magical symbols:	orb, equal armed cross, the shepherd's crook, the sceptre

Also called Gedulah. As Chokmah is the all-begetting Father, Chesed is the all-protecting Father. The energies of Chesed are similar in many ways to the God Jupiter, beneficial and protecting if it suits his propose. Chesed is the sphere of constructive ideas.

Chesed is the architect of city-states, from Atlantis to Rome. Chesed is also the first Sephira in the Ethical Triangle.

Geburah

Translation:	Strength
Astrological:	planet Mars
Archangel:	Khamael
Order of angels:	Seraphim (Fiery Serpents)
Colour on Queen scale:	red
Divine name:	Elohim Gibor
Magical symbols:	the pentagon, the five petaled rose, the sword and spear, the scourge

Truth is, Geburah is not the easiest Sephira to understand. Universal law dictates that everything is in a state of continual change, from the microcosmic spinning of atoms, to the macrocosmic rotation of the Solar system around our Sun. All things are in motion, winter to summer, hot to cold, the ebb and flow of the tides of the seas, and the ages of humanity march ever forward.

Geburah does not work through an earthquake or flood. That phenomenon is due to the activity of cosmic forces that are way beyond the control of Gods and men!

But it is in how we deal with the aftermath of disaster, that concepts of Geburah become evident. The main function of Geburah is to restore the status quo, creating order out of chaos. If breaking a few heads is required, so be it.

To make a fruit tree bear good fruit, a hard pruning back is usually necessary. Chesed will build cities and Geburah will pull them down once they have become decadent and corrupt, falling in on themselves when they have outgrown their original function. Sadly, new things are not born without a small amount of blood and pain.

Mars is the astrological planet of Geburah and is named after Mars the Roman god of war. Mars is one of the most powerful tools in arsenal of Geburah. With joyous zest Mars will rage and war until the power of Chesed will start the building process once more leading to a period of peace and restoration.

Tiphareth

Translation: Beauty
Astrological: Sun
Archangel: Raphael
Order of angels: Malachim (Kings)
Colour on Queen scale: yellow
Divine name: Eloah ve Daath
Magical symbols: truncated pyramid, calvary cross, rose cross, and cube

Tiphareth sits in the middle of the Tree of Life on the pillar of Mildness. Its astrological planet is the Sun, and similarly to our own Sun, it brings harmony and balance to the spheres that orbit around it. Without the loving influence of Tiphareth, Chesed and Geburah would be out of control.

Like all the Sephiroth on the middle pillar, Tiphareth expresses our deep desire to step out of our heavy cloak of the personality to embrace are true spiritual nature. We might not embrace Kether directly but through the medium of Tiphareth we can embrace the God or Goddess within ourselves.

Interestingly, Stewart Farrar in his book *What Witches Do* postulates the idea that esoteric religions can see no higher than Tiphareth. Take Christianity, for example. The Christ figure is located in the centre of Tiphareth symbology as the redeemer, along with other sacrificial Gods. Having found their chosen one, the religious seeker is happy to bask in the golden glow of Tiphareth, reasoning that the remaining two Sephiroth in the Ethical Triangle, Geburah and Chesed, are a dualistic union of pagan ideology representing

3. The ten Sephiroth in descending order

Mars and Jupiter, Strength and Honour, and best left alone.

Similarly, outside of their remit are the three Sephiroth: Kether the unknowable, Chokmah the all-begetting father, Binah the Mother Goddess, which make up the Supernal Triangle. Union with Tiphareth and their Holy Guardian Angel is enough to satisfy the true believer, but not the true magician!

I personally can see this course of action as a reasonable stance to take. Why would certain individuals need to travel beyond the realm of Tiphareth once they had achieved their personal goal to become one with their inner Christ child, Holy Guardian Angel or particular spiritual and religious objective?

However, there are persons out there willing to reach out beyond the blinding light of faith to walk into the unknown. This is the domain of madmen, poets and magicians, so have fun!

Netzach

Translation: Victory
Astrological: planet Venus
Archangel: Haniel
Order of angels: Elohim (Gods)
Colour on Queen scale: green
Divine name: Jehovah Tzabaoth
Magical symbols: the girdle, the rose, and lamp

Netzach is the realm of the emotions, of animal instincts, and the group mind. Like Binah and Chokmah, but on a lower level (plane) Netzach balances with its opposite Hod, as force and form.

The Sephira Netzach is peopled by elusive beings hovering around the frontiers of manifestation, like its divine angelic order name, Elohim (Gods) confirms.

Netzach is the first Sephira in the Astral Triangle. its concepts are less abstract, not quite material, but real enough in their own way.

Netzach, the seventh Sephira, with its rose temple to Venus and its beautiful garden setting could be a facsimile to the garden of Eden. It holds the key to the underlining power of the seven divine principles, contained in the seven Lamps of Power.

Hod

Translation:	Glory
Astrological:	planet Mercury
Archangel:	Michael
Order of angels:	Beni Elohim (Sons of Gods)
Colour on Queen scale:	orange
Divine name:	Elohim Tzabaoth
Magical symbols:	names and versicles and apron

Hod is the Sephira of reason and logical thought. The Egyptian God associated with Hod is the ibis-headed God Thoth, the god of the written word inspired by the characters seen in the patterns birds make when they fly in formation across the Nile.

To build a cathedral you need to calculate weights and measures, and furthermore to be able to see the beauty in mathematics that is made manifest in the final structure. The Hodic mason sees beauty and feels emotion in the perfect arch as a person of a Netzach nature sees beauty in the perfect flower.

To calculate the motion of the planets and plot the course of the Sun though the starry vault of the Zodiac is joy of the Hodic mind. They may live and work in an ivory tower, but through the eye of their telescope explore God's garden in the heavens. Tell me that's not magical!

Yesod

Translation: Foundation
Astrological: Moon
Archangel: Gabriel
Order of angels: Cherubim (the Strong)
Colour on Queen scale: violet
Divine name: Shaddai El Chai
Magical symbols: perfume and sandals

Yesod purifies the energy of the Sephiroth above, like you would purify your magical circle or temple.

Yesod's energy also proves and corrects them, and is responsible for unity of design. This is the final stage before all emanations are transmitted to the physical plane.

This is the sphere of the Astral plane, the Akashic principle where all images are formed in the universal physical ether, which is the raw material of the Astral plane. Denser then thoughts of the mental plane, but lighter and more flowing then the element of water, it forms an organic link between the two. Yesod is the first Sephira that you will contact as you begin to learn to rise on the planes. Any act of opening up higher levels of consciousness will find you entering the world of the Astral.

Yesod also holds the secret of the Moon sphere, and like the Moon is always in a condition of ebb and flow, or cyclic flux. The practise of witchcraft has an important bearing on all magical ope-ration concerning the Moon. With this rhythm, the operations of both the goddess Diana and the fertile goddess Isis are seen.

Yesod is the centre of *the Witches' Pyramid*. If there was a Sephiroth dedicated to Wicca, it would be Yesod.

Yesod's divine name is Shaddai El Chai, Almighty Living God, however, it could equally be translated as Almighty Living Goddess.

It is logical that the Almighty has a dual gender. Do not be indoctrinated into thinking that the universe is male dominated. It is not, nor is it female dominated.

All the ten Sephiroth have a negative side, a vice, if you like, and Yesod's big vice is illusion. Many that reach out and touch the wonders that Yesod can bestow fall foul of this phenomenon. Slowly, the seeker is illuminated from within, and all the mysteries of magic and the gods become clear. The supple and obliging astral fluid will build around them all the proof they need. How often are these words spoken: "I don't need to read books or listen to others, the Goddess has shown me all the wonder of her Empire, for I am one of her chosen ones!"

Some, unfortunately, can stay in this state for a lifetime, adding fantasy upon fantasy. The glamour of Yesod casts a very convincing spell of self-delusion.

Blind faith is aptly named

The answer to this problem is to be pre-armed. Knowing beforehand the pitfalls of the vice of Yesod can help. Always move forward, once you are on the way to the Sephira Hod via the 30th path. The path will shed the light of the Sun into your mortal self, and the desire to study and learn will rush back to fill the void left when you leave your sea of dreams. But fear not, the wonder of Yesod will remain.

Malkuth

Translation: Kingdom
Astrological: Earth
Archangel: Sandalphon

3. The ten Sephiroth in descending order

Order of angels: Ashim (Souls of fire)
Colour on Queen scale: citrine, olive, russet, black
Divine name: Adonai ha-Aretz
Magical symbols: magic circle, the Triangle of Art, altar of the double cube, equal armed cross, the Bride of the Microprosopus

The spiritual experience of Malkuth is the vision of the Holy Guardian Angel. It is only in the sixth Sephira Tiphareth that the vision is rewarded with union with the aforesaid Guardian Angel.

One must be grounded properly before invoking the divine light, particularly at the close of a pathworking. Without the safe guard of returning to the Temple of Malkuth, you could be seriously thrown out of balance.

The Sephira of Malkuth houses the temple of the Earth. It is there to pay homage to the mind-blowing diversity of the planet in which we live. With its ten black pillars shot through with gold, it stands firm and solid on its dais. You might think it is a place of worship, and yes indeed, it is a sacred structure, but it has more in common with a railway station then with a church, because it is the starting point for your journey up the Tree of Life, and your final destination when you wish to return.

So, to sum up, there is only one way onto the Tree of Life, and only one way back and that is through the gates of the Temple of Malkuth. Be amazed.

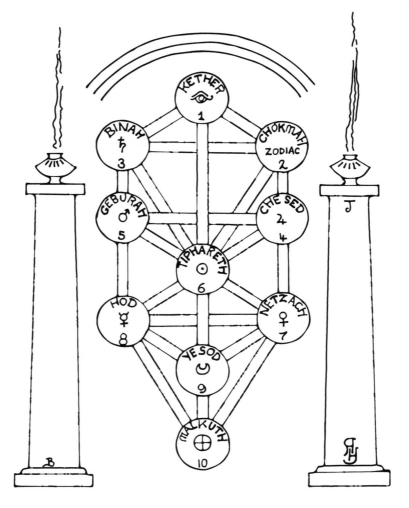

Tree of Life.

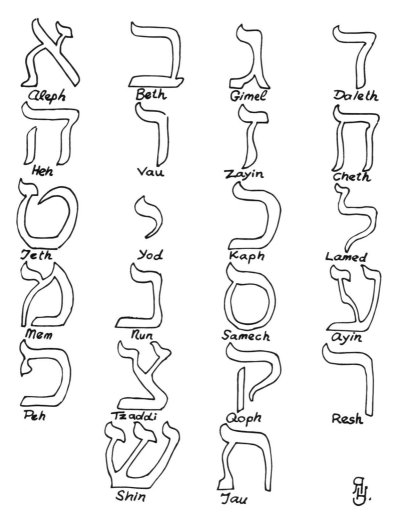

The 22 letters of the Hebrew alphabet.

Ten fascinating things about the Sephira

1. Kether

A strange feeling of well-being when you look up at the night sky and realise that you are just a speck of dust, but a speck of dust that can look upon eternity. All Hail the big scary concept!

2. Chokmah

Be alive, enjoy the boundless freedom of energy of a God unfettered. All Hail Pan!

3. Binah

Lose yourself in the protection of the universal womb, grow and be ready to emerge like a firefly from a chrysalis. All Hail Juno!

4. Chesed

Feel the love, baby! The All-Father has built a citadel on Earth as your personal playground. Don't despise money and it will flow through your fingers. All Hail Jupiter!

5. Geburah

Weak! Not anymore. Arm yourself with fortitude and ride out to face the world in your golden chariot. All Hail Mars!

6. Tiphareth

Oh my, you've just realised what an amazing creature you are, part mortal, part angel, and all parts made by God. All Hail Apollo!

7. Netzach

Those sacred lamps will guide and empower you through the wonderful gardens of the Gods. Love will conquer all. All Hail Venus!

8. Hod

I've got an idea! And Thoth is writing it down. The world turns on such ideas. Mercury moves at the speed of thought, so hitch a lift. All Hail Mercury!

9. Yesod

My love for the Moon Goddess is being returned, the shining path is open to me. Put on your silver sandals, more forward and be blessed. All Hail Diana!

10. Malkuth

I stand on the threshold of the living world and the realms of the spirit and I never felt more alive. All Hail Demeter!

Learn and practise the exercises of balance and purification well before you start working the paths and the experience of the Sephiroth they connect with. Study the Hebrew letters so you will be able to visualise them when you encounter them on any given path.

4. 25th pathworking: Yesod to Tiphareth

What a path, what ambition! In this pathworking you work the most amazing piece of alchemy within the confines of your own body!

Aleister Crowley changed the name of the 14th tarot card Temperance, preferring to call it Art. The Art that Crowley is talking about is the Art of alchemy, were the power of the Odic force and the solar essence of your Tiphareth centre mix in the retort of your body with explosive results, Moon personality changing to Higher Self Sun. Philosopher's Stone is the ultimate goal of alchemy.

The astrological symbol of the 25th path is Sagittarius the archer (mutable fire). Sagittarius is associated with Chiron the Centaur, half-man, half-horse, intellect and strength. Chiron is probably the most famous centaur.

The story of Aesculapius is one example of Chiron's legends.

Thessalian Princess Coronis bore the god Apollo a child, a demigod who was named Aesculapius. On his mother's deathbed, the infant was entrusted to the charge of Chiron, the wisest of centaurs, who was instructed by Apollo and the Moon Goddess Diana in hunting, medicine, music, and the art of prophecy. Aesculapius, when grown up, became a renowned physician. In one instance he even succeeded in restoring the dead to life.

Pluto, the God of Underworld, resented this feat of supernatural skill. The dead belonged to him after all. He complained bitterly to his brother Jupiter. To pacify his brother, Jupiter struck the bold physician down with a lightning bolt. Because Apollo was Aesculapius' father, Jupiter received him into the number of the gods.

This story reinforces the importance of Chiron's position in his role as a guide and teacher in the affairs of man and gods. There are also stories of Chiron helping to arrange divine weddings between mortals and Gods.

A second example of centaur Chiron acting as a guide is the story of Jason's quest for the golden fleece.

Jason commissioned the building of the famous ship Argo, bringing together a band of heroes and demigods to sail to the end of the known world in search of the Golden Fleece. The chart used by Jason to help them find their way was penned by the centaur Chiron.

The conclusion of a poem by Ovid about Jason's journey mentions Chiron's map: "And in the extended keel, a lofty mast upraised and sails full swelling; to the chiefs unwanted first, now they learnt their bolder steerage over ocean and wave, led by the golden objects. Now stars, as Chiron's art had marked the sphere celestial."

Introduction
Yesod to Tiphareth

Hebrew letter: Samekh, meaning tent peg
Astrological sign: Sagittarius, the deliberate interchange of fire and water
Tarot card: Temperance
Esoteric title: the Daughter of the Reconcilers, the Bringer Forth of Life

Samech 25 path

Hebrew letter Samekh.

51

Temperance

Before we can start our adventure on the 25th path, we need to rise up the Tree from Malkuth. To this end we will invoke the Temple of Malkuth.

Create for yourself a ritual space you feel safe and secure in. When you are comfortable, balance yourself up with the Cabalistic Cross exercise.

25th Pathworking

Visualise the Temple of Malkuth.

    We are standing on a round raised dais. Around us are ten black pillars shot through with gold. The floor of the temple is constructed from black and white flagstones like a chessboard. In the centre is a double cubic altar upon which sits an open brass lamp. Its flame rises tall and bright from its centre. When we look up, the pillars soar high above us, their tops lost in a violet mist. Gazing into the flame on the altar we offer up a prayer to the Archangel Sandalphon.

In answer to our prayer, the flame elongates into the form of Sandalphon.

She stands before us, her snow-white wings folded on her back. Her robes of citrine, olive, russet, and black hang sensually around her perfect body.

We ask Sandalphon for her blessing and if she can help us to rise on the Tree to gain admittance to the path of Samekh.

Sandalphon answers: "To reach your goal, follow Yesod, your guide."

With this advice Sandalphon lowers her slender hand over her centre, her lower stomach. We do likewise, meditating on the power of Yesod. A violet ball of energy spins out, enveloping our body in a violet bubble.

Our feet leave the checked floor as we rise up past the ten pillars into the violet mist. Our psychic elevator sets us down before the silver doors of the Temple of Yesod. As the last of the violet mist clears, we place our hands on the cold metal and intone the words of power: 'Shaddai El Chai'.

The silver doors swing inwards and we step into the Temple of Yesod.

The internal walls are built of white marble and follow the contours of the round temple. Standing away from the walls and forming a second circle are nine white pillars shot through with violet. The floor is inlaid with deep blue tiles. Passing though the inner circle of pillars we discover a round pool raised up from the floor. The pool is full to the top with midnight blue water. Looking at the water we can see the full Moon reflected on the surface. Looking up into the lofty domed roof we can't see any sign of the Moon.

In the Temple of Yesod you will only see the Moon's reflection, never the Moon itself.

Floating above the surface of the pool is the temple's Luna lamp. It is a simple hammered silver bowl from which rises the lunar flame. As we gaze into the lunar flame it grows into a human shape that transforms into the Archangel Gabriel. His wings are silver, edged with violet lights. His gown is sea green. The sound of distant sea fills the air. Gabriel greets us with a smile, then, turning, he points to three tarot cards that have materialized behind the Moon pool.

We thank Gabriel and walk around the pool to stand in front of the three tarot cards.

On the left-hand side is the major card The Sun, in the middle is Temperance, and on the right, The Star.

These tarot cards are the keys to the 30th, 25th, and the 28th paths. It is the one in the middle that we need, Temperance.

The card shows a female angel pouring liquid from one jug into another. As we concentrate on Temperance, she opens her wings and disappears, leaving in her place an oasis with a pool in the fore-ground. Stepping into the scene we find ourselves standing ankle deep in water. We find that the path has clothed us in white loose-fitting robes that hang down to our knees. Looking around, we see that the pool is surrounded by slender willows, their branches hanging down with their tips touching the surface of the water, like delicate fingers. Everything including ourselves is bathed in silver light from the ghostly moon that hangs low on the horizon shining through the trees. Lotus flowers float on the surface of the pool. Their petals glow like pearls.

Temperance steps out of the willows onto the bank. She tips liquid from one jug to the other. One jug is made of silver, the other is made of gold. Catching our eyes, she smiles and kneeling down, places the silver jug onto the surface of the pool. It floats half submerged and glides towards us.

Temperance places her index finger to her lips in the sign of silence. She turns and disappears back through the willow trees taking the golden jug with her. As we wade towards the semi submerged jug, the pool becomes deeper as the water closes over our hips. A centaur appears on the bank where Temperance stood minutes before. He rises up his bow and fits an arrow. His aim is true, and he hits the silver jug, tipping its contents into the waters.

Before the jug has chance to slip under the water, we reach down and scoop it up. The liquid contained in the silver jug has an amazing effect on the waters: they start to bubble and boil and glitter like a moonlit cauldron. This reaction manifests as the Odic force (a sexually charged form of astral energy.)

This sexual dynamo drives all living things into being, embraced by the Astral pool and blessed by the Moon: oh, sacred lust and abandonment!

With the sacred silver jug full of Odic liquid now safely in our hands, we wade to the far bank and up into the surrounding willows. We follow the same path that Temperance took, out though the small oasis. Two pomegranate trees stand on either side of the path like sentinels. The path is well worn by the many that have gone before.

The path leads us out onto a sea of sand. A great desert stretches before us, lit by the first ray of the rising sun. The full moon dips behind us like a pale pearl. The golden Sun clears the salmon pink horizon. The view before us comes into sharp relief lit by the new dawn. Our path leads to an oasis of olive trees. Someone has set up a camp by the well at the centre. A large red and white canvas tent dominates the scene. As our stony path gives way to soft sand, we trudge towards the camp.

Holding the jug close to our chest so we don't spill a drop of its precious liquid, we trudge up to the oasis.

The tent has been pitched in the middle of the olive grove. The tent flaps had been tied back to form an entrance, the folds so arranged as to create the Hebrew letter Samekh, which is apt, as one of its meanings is the tent peg.

We step though the mouth of Samekh into the body of the tent. The floor of the tent is covered in brightly coloured rugs. The back section of the tent is rolled up so we have an uninterrupted view out to the east and the newly risen sun. An iron tripod stands in the middle of the tent. It supports a large bowl made of a strange alloy of bronze with gold veins. We are not sure: could it be electrum?

Sweet-scented incense rises from its bed of red hot charcoals. The light from the Sun is so bright we did not notice the Lady Temperance standing in the shadows. She moves into the sunlight. Next to the incense burner in her hands she holds the gold jug.

We ask her what we should do next.

"I am the keeper of all alchemy, and my name is Art!" says Temperance.

She invites us to pour a little of our liquid onto the hot coals of the brazier. We carefully do so. White steam rises from the bowl mixing with the sweet smell of the incense. Golden rays of the Sun tint the swirling vapour, turning it into a golden white cloud, with flashes of silver lighting running through it. Temperance steps forward and with outstretched arms she thrusts the golden jug into the centre of the cloud. As if by magic the cloud is sucked into the mouth of the golden jug.

Temperance then passes the golden jug to us, saying: "Tip the mixture from jug to jug and be transformed."

Carefully we pour the elixir from jug to jug. We feel a change deep down in the core of the body and mind. The feeling is best *described as a spiritual orgasm, as the physical and spiritual sides of your being struggle to be one. When the feeling becomes overbearing, we tip the mixture onto the hot coals in the brazier. A great mist rises not just out of the bowl, but out of the ground itself. The light is failing as the mist envelops all. Through the mist we can see the Sun and Moon travel across the sky, the Sun is swallowed up as the Moon and Sun embrace. Everything is fading. The tent, incense burner, the oasis – all are lost in the thick clinging cold mist. Suddenly, there we are alone in an infinity of cold oblivion, no warmth, no dimension, no guidance, no gods!*

"If you've never cried, your eyes can't be beautiful" (Sophia Loren)

But there is noise, the sound of hoofbeats on the wind. The Moon parts slowly from the Sun's embrace, and a single shaft of sunlight cuts through the darkness lighting up a centaur, as he races to our aid. The Centaur lifts his bow and releases an arrow that arches high into the heavens, leaving in its wake a rainbow of brilliant colours that reaches down to settle at our feet. This is the rainbow bridge of the 25th path. It seizes our legs and body in its colourful embrace and carries us up and away to set us down before the gates of Tiphareth.

We stand on the top of the world. It is as if we stand at the gates of Olympus itself. Below us is the world split into four quarters like the disc of Malkuth. To the east wind-blown mountains, high places full of beauty, remarkable birds soar in the azure blue firmament. Looking to the south we see the lands of deserts and wide places where the golden lion struts, golden topped pyra-

mids glint in the fierce heat of the Sun, caravans of camels cross the waste land bringing their exotic goods from the ends of the earth. To the west the great oceans circle the earth and great sailing ships plough the waves. To the north we see vast forests stretching their fingers towards the snows of the northern realms bathed in the light of the aurora borealis.

Two herms of Apollo and Daphne guard the way. Between them is suspended a cloth of spun gold. Saying the words of power: 'Eloah ve Daath' we breathe on the surface of the veil. The cloth of gold shimmers and is lifted by a light breeze, allowing us to pass into the inner sanctum of the Temple of Tiphareth.

The structure sits on a large, well-tended lawn which is dotted all over with bright daisies. Six golden pillars shot through with purple stand on a round, raised dais of white marble, their tops joined together by curved lintels forming an upper circle, all decorated to match the columns. We climb up the six steps and walk into the Temple of Tiphareth. In the centre there is a waist high pyramid with the top missing (a truncated pyramid.)

An ornate golden bowl embellished by handles fashioned into cherubs stands on the flat summit of the pyramid. The solar flame rises from the centre of the bowl like a pencil of pure golden light. Surrounding the altar, a mosaic of green laurel leaves adorns the white floor of the dais.

We offer up a prayer of blessing and thanks for arriving safely. In answer to our prayer the flame on the altar rises up to form the figure of the Archangel Raphael, Prince of Brightness, Beauty, and Life.

Raphael blesses us and suggests we return this time to the sanctuary of the Temple of Malkuth. We intone the words of power: 'Adonai ha-Aretz'. The Temple of Tiphareth fades and in its place ten back pillars shot through with gold surround us. The floor

of black and white tiles supports us. The double cubic alter bearing the sacred flame stands before us.
  Take a deep breath and let it fade and disappear.

After the pathworking it is nice to ground yourself with a little food and drink.

5. 26th pathworking: Hod to Tiphareth

You can't sell your soul to the Devil,

it's not yours to sell. It belongs to God.

But beware, the Devil will play around

with it for a while, given half a chance.

Devil means Little God.

Every witch I've ever meet seems to be in one mind about the nature of the Devil. They believe the Devil is a Christian concept, someone for the Christians to blame when one of their flock steps out of order thus breaking their strict code of moral behaviour.

Witches reason that they don't worship the Devil, as it's a Christian deity, and Wicca is not a Christian religion.

However, although witches profess that they don't worship the Devil, we are most certainly on nodding terms with him. If you've been lucky enough to have visited Boscastle Witchcraft museum in Cornwall, you would have found in amongst the artefacts from our recent and distant past many images of the Devil, from lurid pictures on printed cards to figurines and all manner of Devil related paraphernalia.

This passion for the darker side of the path is usually harmless, manifesting itself in Halloween celebrations and the odd black candle. But all these concepts help colour our understanding of the 26th path, and more importantly ourselves.

Give the Devil his due?

The horned God of the Witches is certainly not the Christian Devil, rather a benevolent nature spirit that rules over the land and animal kingdom alike. The Horned God is also a caring and devoted consort to the Moon/Earth Goddess. As well as his role as Lord of the Witches, he brings fertility and blessings on his followers.

The Christians stole the image of the Horned God from the old Pagan religion, and made him the Devil of their new religion. Take the great god Pan for example. Then look at the popular image of the Christian Devil, and compare the image to Pan. There can be no argument; the above practise of undermining beliefs of others is unashamedly true.

So how do we approach the 26th path? Do we see the Devil on the major tarot card as lord of evil and tempter of humankind? Or rather a representation of our beloved Horned God?

It is almost certain that The Devil card, key fifteen in the original tarot symbolism, was meant to represent the Christian Devil, and was meant to represent evil incarnate.

In the past, European Christians were gripped with religious paranoia: would the Devil steal your soul or that of your friends and family?

These fears were real enough in the minds of simple working people, and happily reinforced by the Church that waged open war on the Devil and all his work. We are all familiar with the European witch hunts and all their gruesome exploits.

Therefore, through the 26th pathworking, we learn to understand the nature of temptation, and the excesses of greed and selfish desire whose epicentre is represented by the Devil Card.

But this Devil also shows us the way to liberate ourselves from the drudgery of being always on a guilt trip! As we reach the end of the path, the Devil is transformed into the god Pan, who shows us a way to free ourselves by following in the enlightened ways of our forefathers, free from guilt, but aware of our responsibility to each other and to the planet we all share.

Many put forward the concept that the Devil represents the material world, telling us that the material world we are born into is a sinful illusion, there to prepare us for the glorious afterworld, Heaven and similar notions. "Come tomorrow, you will get your reward in heaven" etc. This seems to be a general concept with all major religions that you will get your reward in heaven or the afterlife, but never today!

In the East the idea of reincarnation is well established and appeals to many of the Wicca. But again, the idea that you are caught up in a round of reincarnation to polish and perfect your soul until you have reached a level where you can leave the cycle of death and rebirth and be free of the material world at last, seems a laborious process at best.

I personally like the idea of reincarnation, however, what is so wrong about the material world I was born into? This surely is the world of Malkuth the Kingdom, the final goal. All life is here, the birds and bees, trees and flowers, and all creatures under the Sun, the oceans, and seas and all the abundance therein. For me to be a Pagan is to embrace life and not wish for death, with the thin promise of a better life on the other side.

On the theme of life being an illusion. In the twentieth century there was a magician called Madeline Montalban who, when not busy in ritual, held group sessions for those interested in the occult. In her early life Madeline was afflicted with polio and never really enjoyed good health and was frequently in pain. At one of these meetings everyone was sat around the table consulting the tarot cards. A woman at the session declared to Madeline Montalban, when Madeline complained about pains in her legs, that pain was just an illusion, and she should rise above it. Madeline promptly kicked the woman hard in the shin. The woman cried out in pain and turned on Madeline saying: "Why did you do that?!" Madeline answered: "I thought you said pain was just an illusion!"

The point I am trying to make is, it's all well and good to talk about whether or not the whole life thing is real or imaginary, but when life is kicking your shin, it's hard to ignore it.

Some deliberations on The Devil Card

In gematria the Biblical phrase: 'Theos eini epi gaia' (I am God on Earth) has the numerology value of six, six, six.

In some early tarot packs, The Devil is shown wearing asses' ears instead of horns. The asses' ears could be a reference to the Roman God Priapus, god of the phallus to whom the ass was said to be offered up as a sacrifice. The sexual connotations are obvious.

Aleister Crowley took the notion that the Devil card is phallic one step further. He said the card transcended all limitations. The Devil in Aleister Crowley's celebrated Thoth pack shows a large erect phallus with the image of a white goat superimposed over the top. The goat has a third eye, which refers to the Hebrew symbol Ayin, the eye. The goat has a dual meaning, firstly it's the sign of Capricorn exalted in the heavens, and secondly Pan, whom Crowley calls Pan Pangenetor, the All-Begetter.

The other name associated with the Devil is Baphomet.

According to Aleister Crowley, Baphomet is a form of bull-

-slaying God, connected to Mithras, and rumoured to have been worshipped by the Knights Templars as an ass-headed deity. Aleister Crowley furthermore associates Baphomet with the desert Egyptian god Set, and also with Satan and Saturn.

Interestingly, the early Christians were accused of worshipping an ass-headed god, connected with the wild ass of the wilderness, and identified with Set, Satan and Saturn: a scary thought.

In the play *Midsummers Night Dream*, William Shakespeare created a lovable character called Bottom the Weaver. In the play Bottom is turned into an ass-headed lover of Titania, queen of the fairies, by a mischievous spirit called Puck, also called Robin Goodfellow, henchman of Oberon, king of the fairies.

One of the most infamous images of Baphomet was created by the French magician Eliphas Levi. His line drawing appeared in 1855 in his book *Dogme et Rituel de la Haute Magie* (Dogmas and Rituals of High Magic). The image is a construct of the four elements with both male and female attributes. The goat head mask could be a reference to the Goat of Mendes. Eliphas Levi actually named the image '*The Goat of Mendes*'.

The story goes that the Goat of Mendes was a sacred temple goat, utilized in an ancient cult in the city of Mendes Egypt. Supposedly, the goat copulated with the priestess of the temple in certain religious ceremonies.

Sadly however, it seems none of this is factual. The confusion starts with the assumption that the Ram God of Mendes was a goat! Eliphas Levi for reasons best known to himself thought the Ram God was a Goat God. But why spoil a good story?

This image of the Goat of Mendes was graphically brought to life in the orgy scene in the British film *The Devil Rides Out*, also known as *The Devil's Bride* in the United States.

Produced by Hammer Film Productions in 1968 and directed by

Terence Fisher, the film was based on the novel *The Devil Rides Out*, written by the renowned novelist Dennis Wheatley.

The Satanic treatment of the Goat of Mendes in the film only helped to give the image celebrity status in the world of witchcraft and magic, and like *The Wicker Man*, the film has achieved a cult following. One young lady once told me that the scene where the Goat of Mendes appeared in the woods, far from shocking or scaring her, excited her to such a degree that as she left the cinema she was motivated to seek out and join a witches' coven.

Summing up: as I pointed out, witches say they don't believe in the Devil, but most are drawn to the image, which excites them in a way the traditional Horn God does not. Possibly it is the dark side of our natures that needs an outlet. Perhaps the Devil of the Christians stimulates a deeper race memory of the dark horned hunter god of the wild hunt. Perchance, in our hurry to have our Horned God excepted as a wholesome and safe father figure we are attempting to neuter him?

Lucifer is also associated with the Devil. The story says he fell from heaven, having been cast out by God for being too proud, thus taking on the status of a fallen angel and Lord of the World.

Interestingly, the morning star Venus is also referred to as Lucifer. To the Romans the name Lucifer meant Bringer of Light, the illuminator and guide.

Introduction
Hod to Tiphareth

Hebrew letter: Ayin, meaning eye
Astrological sign: Capricorn
Tarot card: The Devil
Esoteric title: the Lord of the Gates of Matter;
the Child of the Forces of Time

Hebrew letter Ayin

The Devil

Before we can start our adventure on the 26th path we need to rise up the Tree from our start place at Malkuth. To this end, we will invoke the Temple of Malkuth.

Create for yourself a ritual space so you feel safe and secure. When you are comfortable, balance yourself up with the Cabalistic Cross exercise.

26th Pathworking

Visualise the Temple of Malkuth.

We are standing on a round raised dais. Around us stand ten black pillars shot through with gold. The floor of the temple is constructed from black and white flagstones like a chessboard. In the centre is a double cubic altar upon which sits an open brass lamp. Its flame rises tall and bright from its centre. As we look up, the pillars soar high above us, their tops lost in a violet mist. Gazing into the flame on the altar we offer up a prayer to the Archangel Sandalphon.

In answer to our prayer, the flame elongates into the form of Sandalphon, Archangel of Malkuth.

She stands before us, her snow-white wings folded on her back. Her robes of citrine, olive, russet, and black hang sensually around her perfect body.

We ask Sandalphon for her blessing and help to rise up the Tree, to gain the 26th path ruled by the Hebrew letter Ayin.

Sandalphon answers: "To reach your goal, follow Hod, your guide."

With this advice Sandalphon lowers her slender hand over her Hodic centre over her right hip. We do likewise and meditate on the power of Hod, and an orange ball of energy spins out, enveloping our body in an orange bubble.

Our feet leave the floor of the temple as we rise up past the ten pillars into the orange mist. Our psychic elevator sets us down before the ice doors of the Temple of Hod.

Reach out, touch the ice doors and intone the words of power 'Elohim Tzabaoth'. The doors swing slowly inwards and we enter the Temple of Hod. Around the edge of a round dais stand eight marble pillars of a red-orange hue shot through with veins of pure gold. They flash a brilliant orange as we move about them. As we look up at the sky, angry red clouds rotate in the heavens. The floor of the Temple of Hod is designed with intricate geometric patterns. In the centre of the temple stands the stone altar, and the front of the stone is carved with the double snakes of the caduceus. On top of the altar sits the sacred lamp of Hod. The flame rises up from a pool of mercury. The altar is flanked by two pillars of fire and water. We focus our gaze on the Hodic flame, which elongates into the form of the Archangel Michael, Prince of Splendour and Wisdom. Michael steps out of the flame and alights onto the floor in front of the altar. He stands before us, his red wings folded neatly on his back. His robe of living fire hangs around his athletic body.

We ask Michael for his blessing and help to rise on up the Tree to gain the 26th path, the path of Ayin.

Michael points behind him, and three tarot cards materialise between four of the pillars. We move around to gaze at the three tarot cards. On the left hand is The Hangman, the one in the middle is The Devil, and the one on the right is The Tower of Destruction.

It's The Devil card we need. This major card shows a picture of the Devil of Christian myth. Two acolytes kneel before him in the act of worship, one male, the other female, both naked and chained to an iron ring set into a block of stone. We look into the face of the Devil. He smiles back with a knowing look.

He stretches out a hairy arm and with his finger beckons to us to follow him. Stepping into the card we find ourselves in a Dickensian cobbled street.

The buildings overhang the street at both sides. It is early evening, the time when twilight romances the senses. Most of the buildings sport quaint shop windows made up from those little glass panes. As shadows deepen, the lights from shop windows entice us to browse their wares. The first window we look into displays chocolates in colourful boxes, and standing proud are chocolate *sculptures decorated with iced roses and violets. Suddenly we feel an overpowering sense of greed and desire. Catching a glimpse of our reflection in the window glass, we are shocked to see a salivating creature looking back. We quickly move on.*

Next door to the chocolaterie is a sex shop. In the window display are naughty nighties in black and satanic red lace. As well as the lingerie there is an impressive selection of sex toys to tempt you into the delicious world of sexual liberation. Walking along the pavement, we find that all the shops sell things we desire, but not necessarily need. Jewellery, designer clothes, holidays to exotic places, expensive wines, all to entice and spoil us and pander to our hedonistic pleasure. The building that entices us the most at this time is not a shop at all, but a pub. A large sign proudly swings above the front doors. On the sign is a picture of a blue parrot with the name below written in gold leaf. Just to finally tempt us, the doors swing inward, throwing an inviting light across the pavement

The interior is warm and friendly, ornamented with polished mahogany and etched glass in typical Victorian style. There is a babble of conversation from the customers that conceal themselves in the shadows. The bar itself is a splendid affair with a brass foot rail running along the floor, and the counter is made of the finest mahogany. The wall behind the counter is mirrored, reflecting the row of optics of spirits and bottles of wine, and more exotic beverages for the more discerning customer. The barman is middle-aged and balding, his apron partly covering a flamboyant red waistcoat. He has a touch of Bacchus about him, with his red cheeks and tipsy nose.

"What's your poison?" he asks.

"A glass of red wine, please," we answer.

"If you find it a bit stuffy in the main saloon, I recommend our beer garden out the back, you can't miss it," suggests the barman.

Suddenly the room does seem rather noisy and heavy with the smell of cigarette smoke which hangs in the air. Taking our glass of red wine with us we pass through the saloon bar and out into the beer garden.

It is a delightful spot. Chinese lanterns hang down from the trees, and grapevines heavy with fruit climb up old brick walls, their bricks partly hidden by lush green vine leaves. Fauns and nymphs sit at the tables drinking wine and eating fruit that is placed in the centre of each of the tables.

They beckon us to sit with them, and we ease ourselves down into their company. A young faun tops up our wine glass from a large jug. When we take a sip, the wine is sweet and delicious. As we drink our wine, all our troubles seem to vanish like a bad dream. Our new--found friends chatter away merrily asking us where we came from, and telling us how beautiful our new horns look! Touching our head, we are not surprised to feel two little horns poking out from the curly hair that has also grown in this strange enchanted beer garden. As we look down, our legs are being trans-formed into goat's legs, and little hooves have taken the place of our shoes. With each sip of your wine we are changing into a faun — or is it a little devil?

The wages of sin are death, but the hours are good.

A gong sounds on the wind and as one, the nymphs and fauns joy-fully leap up and leave the beer garden. They process into a pictur-esque wood that grows behind the pub garden. Grabbing our hand, they take us with them into the centre of the wood. In an open *glade the remains of a ruined temple stand, and flaming torches illuminate the scene. There in all his glory sits the Devil enthroned in the cleft of the Hebrew letter Ayin.*

The fauns lead us into the centre of the grotto and make us kneel before the Devil. An iron chain is looped loosely around our neck, the other end is firmly attached to an iron ring that is set into the ancient temple floor.

Now chained and fully transformed we look up at the baleful apparition before you. We feel afraid. This figure represents the summit of hedonism, the freedom from all responsibility, no more study, no need to follow our spiritual path or any academic process. We are returning to the animal state that is enjoyed by all creatures of the Earth, Air, and Sea, but to do so we sacrifice our own humanity.

A small spark deep inside rebels against our self-imposed imprisonment. We lift our hands and struggle to lift the chain from around our neck. Although the chain is loosely hung around our shoulders, we cannot lift it free, for it was forged by every selfish act, every drunken night, every time we put ourselves first to the detriment of our friends.

The situation is so hopeless we start to smile at the ridiculous state of affairs and our ludicrous transformation, and we start to laugh at the Devil that sits before us. At the sound of our laughter the Devil rises up to his full height, and laughing joins in the joke. We suddenly have the strength to throw off the iron chain.

This simple act of laughing breaks the spell of transformation, and we are ourselves once more. We see the apparition with clear eyes. He is no more the Christian Devil. He has transformed into the great God Pan.

Pan smiles warmly at us and says: "Guilt and fear will soon have you on your knees."

With that, he blows a sweet trill on his pipes and skips into the surrounding woods to chase the enchantment of the night.

Now alone, we look once more at the Hebrew Ayin that the Devil used as a throne. It sits solidly on the stone floor of the ancient temple, its two arms forming a fork. On the top of each is a Hebrew Yod, into which an eye has been carved.

At first, we have the desire to sit in the symbol to prove to ourselves we are no longer afraid. We do so and feel the power of Ayin flowing up through our body, which is then imbued with the power of the all-seeing eye (one of the gifts of the 26th path is the ability to see through illusion).

Armed with our new gift of true sight we can see a golden path drawn out by the rays of the rising sun. The path leads to the of the gates of Tiphareth.

Climbing through the arms of Ayin we make our way down the golden path until we reach two herms of Apollo and Daphne. Between them hangs a veil of spun gold. This is the gateway to Tiphareth. All we need to do is breathe on its surface and utter the words of power 'Eloah ve Daath'. It would be wise at this juncture to return to the Temple of Malkuth, so we intone the words 'Adonai ha-Aretz'.

Visualise the Temple of Malkuth.

We are standing on a round raised dais. Around us are ten black pillars shot through with gold. The floor of the temple is constructed from black and white flagstones. In the centre is a double cubic altar upon which burns an open lamp. Its flame rises tall and bright from its centre. As we look up, the pillars sore high above us, their tops lost in a violet mist.

Offer up a prayer of thanks and let the temple slowly fade in your mind's eye.

6. 24th pathworking: Netzach to Tiphareth

The 24th path connects Netzach to Tiphareth, protected by the Hebrew symbol Nun, and haunted by the spectre of the tarot Major Arcana card Death.

This path must be approached with acceptance to surrender yourself to the lesson of your own mortality. Whatever comes after your current life: heaven or reincarnation, a merry round in the Elysian fields, whatever you perceive your afterlife to be. It is only when you have passed through the initiation of death will you be truly enlightened.

This 24th pathworking is designed to make you think about your own death, and what it means to family and friends when you have passed through that particular fearful portal.

Many cartomancers say that the tarot card Death does not mean death but rather great change, or the end of some aspect of your life. Why can't they accept that people die, and that nine times out of ten the tarot card Death means just that!

Having said that, when you are reading someone's tarot spread you have got to be sensitive. If they get the Death card, I sometimes ask them if they have seen a ghost. If the answer is no, I tell them that they will. If it's their own ghost, it is a bit of a whoops moment.

The card in the Rider Waite pack is more about the angel of death, death riding a pale horse, and all that.

To the ancients the idea of a Lord of Death ruling the underworld made perfect sense. Hades, brother of Zeus, rules the underworld along with his wife Persephone, as does Pluto along with his wife Proserpina in the Ancient Roman religion.

Nevertheless, this underworld is not like the hell of Christians, although many modern films and books would have you believe it is a place of eternal damnation. Hades has many levels. Evildoers were doomed to languish in Tartarus seen as being immeasurably below, where all manner of torments awaited them.

However, if you lived a guiltless life, your soul would be sent to the Elysian Fields, where each met up with their loved ones that have gone before, following their chosen pursuit of their former life. The Elysian Fields are said to be a land of spring, sunshine, happiness and song.

Interestingly, the river Lethe is said to flow through the Elysian Fields, from which those souls who were set to return to earth in new bodies drank oblivion of their former lives. Not quite reincarnation in the Far Eastern rationality, but something quite close.

Homer wrote: "Elysium of the western seas is a happy land, not tried by Sun, or cold, nor rain, but always fanned by the gentle breezes of Zephyrus [God of the West Wind]."

As well as the dreaded Tartarus and the blissful Elysium Fields, there are many levels in between to which us lesser mortal ghosts are sent, a bit like the sorting hat of Hogwarts.

I have not included myths and legends of the afterlife from the vast spectrum of world's religions, from the Norse sagas to the mysteries of China and African tribal beliefs and so on. Obviously, the subject is endless and would swamp this small introduction so I have kept to the Classical Roman/Greek model. But for those of you with a morbid frame of mind, there are countless books on the customs and beliefs of Death.

Bury your thoughts in the graveyard

of occultism and watch them grow!

Introduction

Netzach to Tiphareth
Hebrew letter: Nun, meaning the fish
Astrological sign: Scorpio
Tarot card: Death
Esoteric title: the Child of the Great Transformations,
the Lord of the Gates of Death

Hebrew letter Nun.

Tarot card Death

Before we can start our adventure on the 24th path, we need to rise up the Tree from Malkuth to Netzach. To this end we will invoke the Temple of Malkuth.

Create for yourself a ritual space so you feel safe and secure. When you are comfortable, balance yourself up with the Cabalistic Cross exercise.

24th pathworking

Start by visualising the Temple of Malkuth.

We are standing on a round raised dais. Around us stand ten black marble pillars fashioned in the classical style, shot through with gold veins. The floor of the temple is constructed from black and white tiles like a chessboard. In the centre of the temple stands a double cubic altar upon which sits a brass oil lamp. Its flame rises up from the centre. When we look up, the pillars soar high above us, their tops lost in a violet mist. Contemplating the flame that rises from the sacred lamp we offer up a prayer and blessing to the Archangel Sandalphon.

In answer to our prayer, the flame extends up to form the body of the Archangel Sandalphon.

Sandalphon stands before us, her snow-white wings folded on her back. Her robes of citrine, olive, russet, and black hang sensually around her perfect body.

We ask Sandalphon for her help so we can rise up the Tree of Life to gain the path of Nun, the 24th path.

Sandalphon answers: "Your gateway resides in the Temple of Netzach."

With this advice, Sandalphon lowers her slender hands over her Netzach centre at her left hip. We do likewise, meditating on the power of Netzach. An emerald green ball of light spins out, enveloping our body in a green bubble.

The green bubble of light lifts us up through the tall columns of the Temple of Malkuth setting us down before the gates of Netzach.

We find ourselves standing in a rose garden. A small rose covered temple shaped like a classical Georgian folly stands at the centre of the rose garden. Its domed roof is covered with red Roman tiles. Seven pillars made of green marble shot through with blue and red veins support the domed roof. White doves fly around the rooftop. The door is made of polished copper. In the centre of the door is an emerald set into a silver star. We say the words of power and place our palms on the emerald star: 'Jehovah Tzabaoth'.

The door swings inward allowing us to enter the inner sanctum of the temple.

The first thing we notice is the beautiful smell of rose incense. In the centre is a classical stone altar with the sacred flame burning from the middle of a small pile of burning fruit wood.

Above us in the middle of the domed roof is a smoke hole. Painted around the smoke hole is a seven-pointed star with a lamp suspended from each point. The floor decoration mirrors the ceiling except that each point of the seven-pointed star is set into the floor with colourful mosaic. In the centre of the star is the altar. As we look into the flame its grows and extends into the Archangel Haniel, the female angel of Netzach, called the Princess of Love and Harmony. The swan white wings are neatly folded on her back. Her gown is the finest green silk. Her hair is like burnished copper and hangs over her shoulder. On her head is a circlet of red roses. She blesses us and in return we ask her to show us the way to the path of Nun. As she points behind her, two tarot cards reveal themselves: Death and The Wheel of Fortune. It is the tarot card on the left that we need to follow our chosen path. The image that stands before us is one the most familiar in the tarot deck: Mort, Death, the Grim Reaper.

The card itself represents the dance of death. Its esoteric ti-tle is: the Child of the Great Transformers, the Lord of the Gates of Death.

Stepping though the card we find ourselves in a typical village churchyard. Gravestones surround a pretty village church with a tall steeple, a golden weathercock on its top.

Interestingly, in amongst a group of deep green yew trees grows a small apple tree, sporting an abundance of apple blossom, symbolising Netzach at its most powerful, life-affirming promise of the fruit to come.

As we approach the apple tree, it undergoes a miraculous trans-formation from spring to autumn. Blossoms fall, giving way to swelling fruits that ripen and fall to the ground around the tree, then rot into the grass that circles the small tree. Finally, Boreas the Lord of the North Wind plucks off dry leaves from the tree's branches and carries them aloft.

All this happens in moments. Now the apple tree stands before us bare-boned, its gnawed trunk and bony branches stark against the grey sky.

Before our eyes, the apple tree metamorphoses into a human ske-leton who stands still for a moment, then shakes himself.

"That's better. Life is so exhausting," says Death.

"Now let me show you my realm," he adds.

Death clearly wants us to follow him. He has a strange gait as he walks down the side of the church, keeping to the narrow-paved path.

"Look how peaceful my realm is," Death says proudly. Then he points out some of the more ornate tabletop tombs that fan out from the honey coloured wall of the little church. As we turn around the eastern end of the church, Death stops and leans his skeleton hands on the top of an ancient tabletop tomb. Carved into the front

is the Hebrew letter Nun flanked by two cherubs. Ivy grows up the sides of the old stonework. Death invites us to lay our hands on the top of the tabletop tomb.

"Listen to the voice of your ancestors. They all stand behind you, protecting and watching you," says Death.

We do as we were told and place our hands on the warm stone. Closing our eyes, we listen to the sounds of nature that fill the air: the buzzing of bees, bird calls, the rustle of wind across the tops of the clipped yew trees that add their scent to the roses and wild-flowers that permeates the aura of the place. It is as if Mother Nature was trying to tempt the dead back to life.

From deep inside the tomb we feel the tingle of fear, as we hear the voices of those who have gone before.

"Listen carefully. You might receive a message from beyond the grave," says Death in a melodramatic voice.

We have a feeling that Death is starting to enjoy himself! Our skeleton companion stands up and dances on around the church path. As we turn to follow, Death is nowhere to be seen.

As we scan the graveyard to catch sight of our gruesome guide, we notice sitting on the back of a stone fish, partly submerged in a bed of nodding violets, a tall golden symbol of the Hebrew let-ter Nun. Stepping lightly over the grass we find a small bell hanging from the top of the letter on a purple ribbon. We place our hands on the cool smooth gold and feel the energy of Nun blessing us. We then slip the bell off the symbol and return to the church path. Not sure what to do next, we ring the bell. Its high pitched tone sounds like a warning alarm, which calls to the surrounding trees.

Suddenly, a large raven swoops down and lands on top of an-other tabletop tomb, similar to the one we have just communed with.

The raven has what appears to be a black rose in its beak. Giving us a knowing look, its drops the black rose onto the lime-

stone tomb top. *As we move forward to investigate, the bird flies away. There is an image of a crude skeleton carved into the front of the tabletop tomb, put there no doubt to remind people of their own mortality.*

The skeleton looks strangely familiar. So that's where our gruesome guide disappeared to! And to confirm this idea the skull seems to nod to us. Reaching down we pick up the strange black bloom. A-ha! The flower stings us on the back of our hand. We withdraw our hand sharply and to our horror we realise it is not a black rose but a black scorpion. Its rears up in an aggressive attitude, sting uppermost. As we take a step back, the scorpion scuttles away and disappears down behind the stone tabletop.

The effects of the scorpion's sting quickly take effect. We start to feel light headed. We decide that the best course of action is to make our way back to the church entrance. By this time the poison is starting to make our legs feel heavy. Reaching our goal, we find we are not alone. Grouped outside of the church porch are figures in funeral dress, women in black veils, men wearing tall top hats and black frock coats, all standing around a wooden stretcher draped in black cloth, with a black pillow at its head.

We feel exhausted and just want to lie down. It comes as no surprise when the ushers with a wave of their black gloved hands invite us to lie on the litter. As we lay with our head on the pillow, a feeling of serenity and acceptance descends as we are gently lifted, then carried sedately through the porch into the church. As we travel slowly down the central nave, we are aware that all our friends and family are sitting on the rows of pews, sadly watching us pass. Now is the time for us to reflect on what we have achieved throughout our life. And more importantly, what we could have changed for the better when we had the chance; too late now.

The ushers put us down on two trestles before the altar. High up in the wall behind the altar is a magnificent round stain-glass window (this is called a rose window.) Sun has come out and is shining straight through the rose window in a blaze of colour, projecting a pool of coloured light on the stone floor just in front of the altar. The projection is in a form of a large hexagram, symbol of Tiphareth. The pool of light moves forward to cover our body with its holy light. We feel rejuvenated and slipping off the front of the litter find ourselves standing in the centre of the hexagram. The church and congregation all fade as if a dream.

Before us now stand the herms of Apollo and Daphne holding the golden veil. The gate way into the Temple of Tiphareth lays before us.

All we have to do to enter the Temple of Tiphareth is breathe onto the golden veil and say the words of power, 'Eloah ve Daath'. However, we wish to go no further, and so intone the words of power associated with the Temple of Malkuth, 'Adonai ha-Aretz' and visualise the Temple of Malkuth once more.

The floor of the temple is constructed from black and white tiles, and ten black pillars shot through with gold stand around us. In the centre stands the double cubic altar, on which burns the sacred lamp.

Take a deep breath, and as you exhale, let the temple fade and disappear.

7. 23rd pathworking: Hod to Geburah

Do something amazing on your way
to the scaffold

Some of the legends and stories
associated with the Hanged Man

Legend says that the mighty ash tree Yggdrasil, said by the Norse people to support the whole universe, grew from the body of Ymir, an ancient frost giant slain by Odin and his warriors.

Odin, lord of the Norse Gods, hung on the Yggdrasil the world tree for forty days and forty nights, and there he learnt runes, screaming he learnt them. Furthermore, legend has it that Odin sacrificed one of his eyes in exchange for wisdom. Could Odin be the Hanged Man?

Jesus hung on a wooden cross to save humankind from their own sins. Could it be him?

What about Prometheus the Titan, who was hung by iron chains on a rock, having his liver eaten by an eagle each night only to have it grow back the next day, as punishment for helping humankind defy the Gods, when the element of fire was denied them. Could it be the Titan?

Judas Iscariot is definitely a contender for the roll of the early tarot card The Hanged Man. The image shows the Hanged Man losing thirty pieces of silver from his pockets.

Or he could be just a common criminal, back in Mediaeval

times, baffled (tied) by the heels and hung upside-down, which was a punishment meted out to robbers and debtors.

These and perhaps many more are possible candidates for the role of the Hanged Man.

Some scholars of the classics thought the card to derive directly from the Orphic mystery rites and worship of Dionysus. In ancient times, images of Dionysus were hung in trees to ensure fertility.

The card is said to depict sacrifice in order to achieve regeneration of the land.

A death to ensure fertility in Britain is celebrated in many ways. One such example is the stoning of an effigy of Jack of Lent, or the Lord of Misrule who rules for a day then is ritually sacrificed. This theme of ritual sacrifice appears in the cult movie *The Wicker Man*.

Lent is a Christian festival observed in March and, like Easter, its date varies from year to year. Later in the year, Saturnalia and the winter carnival are examples of customs and beliefs associated with the Winter Solstice, death and regeneration.

Are you willing to suffer to learn?

Introduction

Hod to Geburah

Hebrew letter: Mem, one of the three mother letters meaning water

Astrological sign: Leo

Tarot card: The Hanged Man

Esoteric title: the Spirit of the Mighty Waters, Baptism of the element of water

Hebrew letter Mem

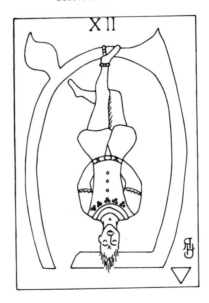

The Hanged Man

Before we can start our adventure on the 23rd path, we need to rise up the Tree from Malkuth. To this end we will invoke the Temple of Malkuth.

Create for yourself a ritual space where you feel safe and secure. When you are comfortable, balance yourself up with the Cabalistic Cross exercise.

23ʳᵈ **pathworking**

Visualise the Temple of Malkuth.

We are standing on a round raised dais. Around us stand ten black marble pillars shot through with gold. The floor of the temple is constructed from black and white flagstones like a chessboard. In the centre is a double cubic altar upon which sits an open brass lamp. Its flame rises tall and bright from its centre. When we look up, the pillars soar high above us, their tops lost in a violet mist. Gazing into the flame on the altar we offer up a prayer to the Arch-angel Sandalphon.

In answer to our prayer, the flame elongates into the form of Sandalphon. She stands before us, her snow-white wings folded on her back. Her robes of citrine, olive, russet, and black hang perfectly around her body.

We ask Sandalphon for her blessing and if she can help us to rise on the Tree to gain the path of Mem, the 23ʳᵈ path.

Sandalphon answers: "To reach your goal, follow Hod, your guide."

With this advice, Sandalphon lowers her slender hand over her Hodic centre, over her right hip. We do likewise. As we meditate on the power of Hod, an orange ball of light spins out enveloping our body in a vivid orange bubble.

Our feet leave the checked floor as we rise up through the ten pillars into the orange mist. Our psychic elevator sets us down be-fore the ice doors of the Temple of Hod. As the last of the orange mist clears, we place our hands on the cold ice and intone the words of power: 'Elohim Tzabaoth'.

The doors swing slowly inwards and we enter the Temple of Hod. Around the edge of a round dais stand eight marble pillars of a red-orange hue shot through with veins of pure gold that flash a brilliant orange as we move about them. As we look up at the sky, angry red clouds rotate in the heavens.

The floor of the Temple of Hod is designed with intricate geometric patterns. In the centre of the temple stands the stone altar. The front of the stone is carved with the double snakes of the caduceus. On top of the altar sits the sacred lamp. Its flame rises up from a pool of mercury. The altar is flanked by two pillars of fire and water. We focus our gaze on the Hodic flame, which elongates into the form of the Archangel Michael, Prince of Splendour and Wisdom. Michael steps out of the flame and alights onto the floor in front of the altar. He stands before us, his red wings folded neatly on his back and his robe of living fire hanging around his athletic body.

We ask Michael for his blessing and if he can help us to rise on the Tree to gain the 23rd path, the path of Mem.

The Archangel Michael points behind him. Three tarot cards materialise between four of the pillars. We move around to gaze at the three tarot cards. On the left there is The Hanged Man, the one in the middle is The Devil, and the one on the right depicts the Tower of Destruction.

The Hanged Man is the key we need to open the 23rd path.

We meditate on the card and let it draw us in.

Stepping through the tarot card we find ourselves standing before a still dark lake. The lake is located in the centre of valley surrounded by stone structures. Towers and cliffs stand like ancient megaliths built by the giants of old, but in reality, they are naturally formed by time and artistic whims of wind and rain.

But in such a remarkable place, man has made his mark on the stones, carving religious images from the distant past, dedicated to the old gods of Woden and the Druids. New Christians images attempt to obliterate the older art with carvings of saints and crosses and Christ himself.

Some of the taller, more impressive megaliths are on the far side of the lake. A small wooden boat is conveniently moored close by. Crude stone steps lead us down to the lapping water. We need to cross the lake, so we climb into the boat. On its bow is carved a wooden horses head. In the centre of the boat is a stout mast, and a rope hangs from a runner at the top. Pulling on the rope lifts a rudimentary sail, and we tie the rope off to a cleat. Wind fills the sail, we cast off, and the boat carries us swiftly across the lake to the far bank.

We arrive at the base of a tall rock face with a wide stone shelf at its foot. A set of steps lead down to water. We moor the boat to a carved wooden post.

Climbing out of the boat, we climb up the steps and stand upon the stone shelf looking about ourselves. A few hawthorn trees have managed to take root in the cracks in the stone floor. Interestingly, there is a well about a metre wide, full nearly to the top with black-ish water. Just behind the well is a larger hawthorn tree. Its gnarled boughs are formed in the shape of the Hebrew letter Mem. A looped rope hangs down, tied above to the natural arch. Sitting on the floor, we slip our foot into the loop, as it seems the thing to do!

Then, as if by magic, the tree starts to grow and the rope pulls us gently off the floor. Taking up the space in the middle of the letter Mem we become the hanged man: 'the Sacrifice'.

We feel the power of Mem flowing into us. Mem represents the element of water and calls to the water of the lake, which starts to raise. The waters creep over the stone shelf. Everything is now upside down from our view point, and the waters seem to be coming down, not up. The water slowly covers our head and moving up our body until we are held in its watery embrace.

We are strangely calm; our anxiety and thoughts are stolen by the waters. We have no trouble breathing, and like babies in the womb we are immersed by the spirit of the mighty waters.

Moreover, like Odin, we listen to the voice of wisdom echoing from the vasty deep. After a while, the water starts to recede, and much of it appears to go down the well. The water gently sets us back down on the rocky shelf under the hawthorn tree gallows. We slip the rope from off our foot and stand up looking around and about. Everything is damp, but other than that, all is as before, the little boat bobs about on its moorings. The trees stand as before.

But there is one thing that the waters show us. The world tree Yggdrasil is carved in the stone cliff behind the hanging tree, now shown clearly by the newly dampened surface. Its roots vanish down into the well, into the underworld.

Looking back across the lake, we see standing on the opposite bank the Temple of Geburah. We return to our boat and pull up the sail, and the winds speed us back to the mooring post. We lower our sail, climb out of the boat and walk up to the iron gates of the temple. The surface of the gates is decorated with heroic figures similar to the image you would see on a Greek urn. As we wish to enter the Temple of Geburah, we place our hands on the iron doors and intone the words: 'Elohim Gibor'.

The Temple of Geburah is built on a raised dais. The floor of the temple is constructed from brick red mosaic, into which has been worked a huge pentagram of green jade tesserae.

Fire red pillars shot through with iron stand between the points of the pentagram. In the centre of the pentagram is the pentagon formed by the lines of the pentagram. Here stands the altar. It is a strange device: two bronze hunting dogs sitting up back to back. A simple hammered out iron bowl sits firmly on their four ears. From the iron bowl rises the Martial flame. It rises up like a pencil of red neon light.

Above our head is the starry vault of heaven swimming in an ocean of indigo eternity. That is Binah.

As we gaze into the flame on the altar, the ruby flame elongates into the figure of the Archangel Khamael. Khamael is dressed like a Roman or Greek warrior. He is young in appearance, but ageless. His wings are small and dove-like, tinged with red.

We bow to the angel that stands before us, and offer up a small prayer to Khamael, Prince of Strength and Courage. He in turn blesses us.

As we do not wish to travel further up the Tree right now, we thank the Archangel Khamael, and utter the words of power to allow us to return to the Temple of Malkuth: 'Adonai ha-Aretz'.

Now visualise the Temple of Malkuth.

The floor of the temple is constructed from black and white tiles, and ten black pillars shot through with gold stand around us. In the centre stands the double cubic altar, on which burns the sacred lamp.

Take a deep breath, and as you exhale let the temple fade and disappear.

Summing up: do embrace the experience of the Sephirotic Temple of Geburah, if you so desire, which after all is the prize gained for having travelled your chosen path. But its unwise at this time to try and move up out of the Witches' Hexagram to explore the Supernal Triangle at the top of the tree. First you need to have fully explored the six paths of the Witches' Pyramid, also called the Astral Triangle, combined with the eight paths of the Witches Hexagram also called the Ethical Triangle, before you are equipped to ascend to the summit of the Tree of Life.

Secondly, I have only included the pathworkings attaining to the middle section of the tree, so unless you have written your own set of pathworkings attaining to the final eight paths of the Supernal Triangle, the safest option is to return to the Temple of Malkuth using the formula of visualisation and the vocal incantations of the word of power and divine name 'Adonai ha-Aretz', as laid down in this book.

8. 22nd pathworking: Tiphareth to Geburah

The Bible tends to be judgmental, so the first judgment is taken from Genesis, the story of Adam and Eve and the garden of Eden. We use these names for our star-selves Adam and Eve Kadmon (heavenly man and heavenly woman.) We become the Tree of Life in its microcosmic form, the bride and groom of the cosmos.

In the story, Adam is the first man created by God from dust, perhaps star dust?

Adam is placed in the garden of Eden, a perfection of Mother Nature before the fall. The paradise garden of Eden is said to be located in the Sephira of Netzach. Adam yearns for a partner and takes a rib from his body thus creating Eve, the first woman. No-thing is perfect, not even in paradise. God, on a whim or for some mystical reason best known to himself, bans the couple from eating the fruit of knowledge from the Tree of Life, warning that the punishment for breaking God's rule was death. Eve can't resist the temptation to try the fruit, and even with God's threat hanging over her she succumbs with a little helpful advice from a serpent, and she eats the fruit. Adam follows suit and the two of them are banished from Paradise. The point here is: why didn't God carry out his threat?

Perhaps judgment prevailed. God had to choose between death and banishment. His first son had changed. He had been touched with the taint of wisdom.

As the story above shows, Justice symbolises one of the four cardinal virtues or moral principles, acclaimed by the ancient stoic philosophers.

Interestingly, ancient Greek society was dominated by men

(although the Goddess Athene, a woman, was patron of Athens).

Men always depicted Justice as a female. The female figure signifying justice is said to be derived from Themis, who married Zeus the sky father. The union bore a daughter named Astraea, now the modern constellation of Virgo. Virgo is the astrological sign of the 20th path, ruled by Yod, and its tarot card is the Hermit. The 20th and the 22nd paths mirror each other on the Tree of Life: Justice by social rule, and Justice by divine intervention.

Introduction
Tiphareth to Geburah

Hebrew letter: Lamed, meaning ox goad
Astrological sign: Libra
Tarot card: Justice
Esoteric title: the Daughter of the Lords of Truth, the Ruler of the Balance

Lamed 22 path

Hebrew Letter Lamed.

Justice

Before we can start our adventure on the 22nd path we need to rise up the Tree from Malkuth. To this end, we will invoke the Temple of Malkuth.

Create for yourself a ritual space so you feel safe and secure. When you are comfortable, balance yourself and cleanse your aura with the Cabalistic Cross exercise.

22nd pathworking

Visualise the Temple of Malkuth.

We are standing on a round raised dais. Around us are ten black marble classic pillars shot through with gold veins running through them. The floor of the temple is constructed from black and white flagstones like a chessboard. In the centre is a double cubic altar, upon which sits an open brass lamp. Its flame rises tall and bright from its centre. As we look up, the pillars soar high above us, their tops lost in a violet mist.

Gazing into the flame on the altar, we offer up a prayer to the Archangel Sandalphon.

In answer to our prayer, the flame elongates into the form of Sandalphon. She stands before us, her snow-white wings folded on her back. Her robes of citrine, olive, russet, and black hang sensually around her perfect body.

We ask Sandalphon for her blessing, and if she can help us to rise on the Tree to gain the 22nd path, the path of Lamed.

Sandalphon answers: "To reach your goal, follow Tiphareth, your guide."

With this advice Sandalphon lowers her slender hand over her heart centre. We do likewise meditate on the power of Tiphareth. A golden ball of energy spins out, enveloping our body in a golden bubble.

Our feet leave the checked floor as we rise up by the ten pillars into a golden mist. Our psychic elevator sets us down before two herms of Apollo and Daphne that guard the way to the inner sanctum of Tiphareth. Between them is suspended a cloth of spun gold.

Saying the words of power: 'Eloah ve Daath', we breathe on the surface of the veil. The cloth of gold shimmers and is lifted by a light breeze, allowing us to pass into the inner sanctum of the Temple of Tiphareth.

The structure sits on a large well-tended lawn which is dotted all over with bright daisies. Six golden pillars shot through with purple stand on a round raised dais of white marble, their tops joined together by curved lintels coloured to match the columns. We climb up the three steps and walk into the Temple of Tiphareth. In the centre is a waist high pyramid with the top missing (trun-

*cated pyramid.) An ornate golden bowl embellished by two cherub-
shaped handles stands on the flat top of the pyramid. The solar
flame rises from the centre of the bowl like a pencil of pure golden
light. Surrounding the altar, a mosaic of green laurel leaves adorns
the white floor of the dais.*

*We offer up a prayer of blessing and thanks for arriving safely.
In answers to our prayer, the flame on the altar rises up to form
the figure of the Archangel Raphael, Prince of Brightness, Beauty,
and Life.*

*Raphael blesses us and points to the three tarot cards hang-
ing in the air behind him: Justice to the left, The High Priestess
in the middle and The Hermit on the right. To gain the 22ⁿᵈ path
it is the tarot card Justice we need.*

*We stand in front of the major card Justice. Displayed on
the card is a queenly woman sitting on a throne. In her right hand is
a cruciform sword and in her left hand she holds the scales of justice.*

*As we gaze at the tapestry, Justice lowers her sword with a flou-
rish, inviting us to walk through a golden arch of living flowers and
fruit. We step into the card and pass into a wonderful garden made
from golden light and rainbow dust that colour the leaves and flowers. Is this the fabled garden of Eden?*

*As the light shifts, it reveals a familiar scene. In a clearing
stands the Tree of Knowledge with its forbidden fruit hanging down
in easy reach. The urge to pick it, to own it, to devour it is so strong
it is almost sexual.*

*We stand transfixed, as an iridescent serpent coils around
the silver trunk. It looks at us with the head of an angel!*

*We would feast on the purple flesh of the fruit ourselves but our
feet seem to be rooted to the spot.*

As we watch, a woman makes her way demurely through

the trees. Although naked, she is bathed in golden light. She is per-
fection with no flaws, and for that matter, no navel! She was never
born, but created fully grown and flawless. She is Eve.
She seems to be having a conversation with the serpent.

Forbidden fruit tastes the sweetest

The rest is the stuff of Biblical legend. Eve's hand reaches up
and picks a fruit and she takes a bite. Adam joins her and, seeing
the purple juice running down her chin, he picks another of the for-
bidden fruit and joins Eve in her rebellion by taking a bite. Igno-
rance is bliss, it is folly to be wise. But too late for that, humanity
is born!

Something goes wrong in paradise?
Doesn't it always!

As Adam and Eve leave the stage, so to speak, the golden gloss
disappears from the woodland garden orchard, driven out by an an-
gry divine wind, leaving in its place a normal English wood full
of deep greens, beeches, oaks, and a lot of brambles. We take
in a deep lung full of damp leaf mould scented air.
This is the first judgment, the first breaking of the law. Interest-
ingly, we are told the punishment for eating the forbidden fruit is
death! But once Adam and Eve had broken the rule of God's law,
it put them outside the law, making them outlaws! The control is
gone. If you don't play by the rules of the game, you are banished
from the board.

8. 22nd pathworking: Tiphareth to Geburah

It is cool under the trees, and a little path winds its way through the trees.

As this is a pathworking, we follow it.

Soon, we come across a large clearing off the right-hand side. In the centre of the clearing is an impressive oak tree. Its boughs stretch out like spokes in a wheel, forming a natural meeting place under their eaves. There seem to be objects hanging from the lowers boughs. Some glint with the promise of gold. We would go and investigate, but next to the mighty trunk stands a large ox! Although it has a garland of woodland flowers around its neck it is obviously a bull. As we contemplate the ox, a body of men dressed is green creep out from the undergrowth and surround us. They are armed with stout staffs. Some have bows drawn, their arrows pointing dangerously in our direction. Stepping forward, their leader takes no time in introducing himself to us: Robin Hood straight out of the films and story books.

"Welcome, strangers," he says as a form of introduction.

He is a mix of Peter Pan and the Greenman. He is interested in our quest for justice and wisdom. Robin and his band of merry followers escaped persecution by returning to nature, and now have more in common with wood elves and dryads.

But like us all they too have rules to live by. Although they are outlaws, they are still bound by the laws of nature and simple survival skills.

We ask: *"Why is there a huge male ox under your oak tree?"*

Robin replies: *"The ox was stolen from a local farmer that helps us out from time to time. The bailiffs claimed that the ox was owed to the Sheriff in lieu of taxes. We managed to steal it back from the soldiers as they passed through the forest. We were going to take it back to the farmer the next day. However, during the night, the forest dryads took a fancy to the ox, hence the garland of flowers.*

This old oak is our treasure tree. We hide our spoils in its boughs, but the ox is drawing attention to it. He won't move. We have tried, but he prefers the adoration of the dryads to pulling the plough back on the farm, so he's happy to stay put."

With a flourish of his hand Robin shows us the treasures that hang in the tree. Strings of beads hang down, golden bangles, purses of coins, all manner of precious things.

Looking up into the tree we are amazed to see a golden Lamed symbol of the 22nd path just hanging there. We have an idea: Lamed is Ox goad.

So, we ask Robin: "If we can persuade the ox to leave the shelter of the oak tree, will you give us safe passage out of the forest?"

Robin Hood replies: "If you can get the ox back onto the path from under our tree, I will show you the way out. But there is one condition: you must take the sword of rightfulness back to the Lady of Justice, where it belongs."

"Why the sword, what is so special about it?" we ask.

"There are so many laws that those who sit in judgment need heavy books of law to keep up. And with such books crafty lawyers that wield them blind the judges from the simple truth. This sword is the daughter of Excalibur. Its two edges confer correction on one side and consecration on the other," explains Robin.

To our surprise the sword is a crude wooden one, like a player in a mummers' play would use. We take the wooden sword nonetheless, slipping it though our belt.

"May we?" we say taking down the golden Hebrew letter Lamed.

Robin nods his head.

We feel the power of the letter Lamed running down our arm and into our body, as the symbol straightens up, the Yod at the top becoming a golden prong.

Brandishing Lamed in our hands we edge our way around the ox and give it a gentle prod in its flanks. The power of the Lamed works its magic and the ox lifts his giant head and moves forward a few paces. Moving from side to side we manage to steer the ox back onto the path and out from the influence of the oak and its hidden dryads.

A gang of Robin Hood's men gather around the ox and with pointed sticks drive the beast down the path and presumably back to the farmer's farm.

Robin stands before us, both hands stretched out, into which we place the golden Lamed. We watch as he hangs it once more back into the boughs of the mighty oak and says: "The best place to hid things is in clear sight." Robin Hood is symbolic of the Fool of the 11th path, and its sacred symbol is Aleph the Ox!

Robin is as good as his word and leads us personally to the edge of the tree line. A dilapidated road runs out across the surrounding countryside.

"It's an old Roman road," explains Robin.

With these final words Robin Hood returns to the trees.
Like old Alfred Watkins' old straight track, the Roman road points the way to a citadel built on the distant hills across a valley of corn fields with small outcrops of regimented trees that could be orchards.

Just as we feel that the idea of a long walk does not appeal to us, a chariot moves quickly down the road towards us.

The charioteer pulls up in front of us. Two horses paw the ground: one black as night, the other milk white. On the front of the chariots car are painted two angels in luscious golds and reds. One is Sandalphon, the other is Metatron. Legend has it that they were the two cherubs that adorned the Ark of the Covenant.

The charioteer flicks the reins and turns the chariot in a full circle so that it points the way back down the road.

"Have you the sword?" asks the young charioteer.

We hold up the wooden sword.

"Hop on board, and hold on tight," says the charioteer.

The platform is more spacious than we would imagine. Holding on to the metal rails that follow the contours of the side of the car we set off at a brisk trot down the ancient roadway or street as the Romans called it.

The countryside speeds by, and we soon pass through the city gates. The chariot comes to a stop in a spacious city square. Directly in front of us is the Hall of Justice. Solid and prosperous, it is more like a city museum than the Hall of Justice.

Alighting from the back of the chariot we thank the driver and step down.

The doors to the building stand open. On entering, we pass down a long hallway, pillars flanking its both sides. Exhibits run down the two walls behind the pillars. We stop to look at an Egyptian frieze of the Goddess Maat sitting in her Chamber of Judgement with a large ostrich feather rising from her headdress. It is said that it quivers each time someone lies.

The first chamber leads us into the main Hall of Justice. Matriarch Justice sits on her throne, built high up on a marble plinth. Two pillars stand at either side of her throne, one red, one blue. A pair of iron doors are set into the marble plinth directly under her throne. Standing before her, we notice that her right hand is empty, and the scales in her left hand are being pulled down by a mischievous monkey dressed in a lawyer's gown.

"Have you the sword?" Justice asks.

We pass it to her. She leans down and takes a firm hold of the hilt. Justice raises the sword up with a flourish, the point facing the heavens. The wooden sword is transformed in a rush of fire into a real sword of steel (hidden in clear sight!) Its twin *edges of correction and consecration blaze with blue and red flames, which dart through her body to pass into the scales she holds in her left hand.*

The monkey, hit by the full force of balance and reason, swings quickly down to the floor and races into the shadows. The Lady of Justice resumes her classic pose, sword up, scales in balance.

"The way to the Temple of Geburah is clear to you," says Justice.

The iron doors set into the marble plinth begin to glow with concealed power. The surface of the gates is decorated with heroic figures similar to the images you would see on a Greek urn. As we wish to enter the Temple of Geburah, we place our hands on the iron doors and intone the words: 'Elohim Gibor'.

The iron doors swing silently inwards.

The Temple of Geburah is built on a raised dais. The floor of the temple is constructed from brick red mosaic, into which has been worked a huge pentagram of green jade tesserae.

Five red pillars shot through with iron stand between the points of the pentagram. In the centre of the pentagram is the pentagon formed by the lines of the pentagram. Here stands the altar. It is a strange device: two bronze hunting dogs sit up back to back, and a simple hammered iron bowl sits firmly on their four ears. From the iron bowl rises the Martial flame. It rises up like a pencil of red neon light.

Above our heads is the starry vault of heaven swimming in an ocean of indigo eternity. That is Binah.

We offer up a prayer to the Archangel Khamael, Prince of Strength and Courage. As we gaze into the flame on the altar, the ruby flame elongates into the figure of the Archangel Khamael. Khamael is dressed like a Roman or Greek warrior. He is young in appearance, but ageless. His wings are small and dove-like with a red tinge. On his breast plate is the image of Medusa.

Khamael blesses us, and we explain that we must at this junc-ture return to the Temple of Malkuth to bring this pathworking experience to an end.

We utter the words of power to allow us to return to the Temple of Malkuth: 'Adonai ha-Aretz'.

The Temple of Malkuth appears before us. The floor of the temple is constructed from black and white tiles, and ten black pillars shot through with gold stand around us. In the centre stands the double cubic altar, on which burns the sacred lamp.

Take a deep breath, and as you exhale, let the temple fade and disappear.

Again, as before with the 23rd pathworking, embrace the experience of the Sephirotic Temple of Geburah if you so desire, which after all is the prize gained for having travelled your chosen path. But its unwise at this time to try and move up out of the Witches Hexagram to explore the Supernal Triangle at the top of the Tree. First, you need to have fully explored the six paths of the Witches' Pyramid, also called the Astral Triangle, combined with the eight paths of the Witches' Hexagram, also called the Ethical Triangle, before you are equipped to ascend to the summit of the Tree of Life.

Secondly, I have only included the pathworkings leading to the middle section of the Tree, so unless you have written your own set of pathworkings for the final eight paths of the Supernal Triangle, the safest option is to return to the Temple of Malkuth using the formula of visitation and the vocal incantations of the word of power and Divine name, 'Adonai ha-Aretz', as laid down in this book.

9. 21st pathworking: Netzach to Chesed

The Wheel of Fortune

The Wheel of Fortune is all about how you fare in life, your ups and your downs. What does it matter what I do: my life is already mapped out by Fate!

This idea of Fate runs deep in the human psyche. The word itself, Fate, is where we get the word fairy, like the evil fairy spinner in Sleeping Beauty that seals our destiny. The Moirae, the triple Goddesses of ancient Greece, spun the destiny of men and women on their early distaffs.

The vice of Malkuth is inertia. Things like to stay where they are. Although the wheel of life turns day in, day out, you remain still in the core of things like the axle at the centre of a wheel. Any attempt to change your situation will be gently resisted. The universe likes things to stay in their place. You can break out, but it takes determination and willpower.

The Hebrew letter Kaph means closed fist. When you meet the palmist who will read your palm, she will persuade you to open your fist and show her your palm. It is apt then that she tells you your destiny.

The Hebrew letter Kaph is a double letter, meaning it has a positive and negative side to its nature. In context of the Wheel of Fortune it symbolises both poverty and riches. You could argue that the concept of earthly possessions is of no importance to your spiritual journey, but your progress through life will be much harder if the dice are loaded against you.

Money has its own special energy, so don't despise it!

The story of the sandal maker

The sandal maker sits outside the front of his shop. He is a young sandal maker taught by his father and his father was taught by his grandfather before him. He spends his day watching the world go by. People travel the world wearing sandals much like his own. One of the meanings of the Egyptian Ankh is the symbol of the sandal strap. Your ankle goes through the loop and its tail attaches to the front of the leather sole. The Ankh as the symbol of the sandal strap means 'Going forth'.

So why does the sandal maker not pick up the Ankh in its sandal form and go forth? The simple truth is he is too afraid to throw himself on to the wheel of fortune. Don't make that mistake of the careful. Be brave, go forth!

The Golden Dawn Tarot has twelve spokes on their tarot card, The Wheel of Fortune, one for each of the twelve signs of the Zodiac. Moreover, they represent the twelve great eons of humanity. We are currently in the Age of Aquarius. The wheel can also be seen as an example of the world religions, each spoke a different creed or faith, all set firmly around a central hub. Each of these religious paths leads to the calm inner temple of truth where the sacred flame burns.

Furthermore, the spoked wheel can be equated to the rays of the Sun around which all life revolves, and could be recognised to represent Tiphareth, golden temple of truth. But again, the tarot card The Wheel of Fortune being symbolic of the golden Sun centre of Tiphareth is a bit of a stretch, although worth mentioning.

Introduction
Netzach to Chesed
Hebrew letter: Kaph, closed hand
Astrological planet: Jupiter
Tarot card: The Wheel of Fortune
Esoteric title: the Lord of the Forces of Life

Kaph 21 path

Letter Kaph

The Wheel of Fortune.

Before we can start our adventure on the 21ᵗʰ path we need to rise up the Tree from Malkuth to Netzach. To this end we will invoke the Temple of Malkuth.

Create for yourself a ritual space so you feel safe and secure. When you are comfortable, balance yourself with the Cabalistic Cross exercise.

21ˢᵗ pathworking

Start by visualising the Temple of Malkuth.

We are standing on a round raised dais. Around us are ten black marble pillars fashioned in the classical style. They are shot through with gold veins. The floor of the temple is constructed from black and white tiles like a chessboard. In the centre is a double cubic altar upon which sits a brass oil lamp. Its bright flame rises up from the centre. The pillars soar high above us, their tops lost in a violet mist. Contemplating the flame that rises from the brass lamp, we offer up a prayer and blessing to the Archangel Sandalphon.

In answer to our prayer, the flame extends into the form of Sandalphon.

Sandalphon stands before us, her snow-white wings folded on her back. Her robes of citrine, olive, russet, and black hang sensually around her perfect body.

We ask Sandalphon for assistance so we can rise up the Tree of Life to gain the path of Kaph, the 21ˢᵗ path.

Sandalphon answers: "Your gateway resides in the Temple of Netzach."

With this advice Sandalphon lowers her slender hands over her Netzach centre at her left hip. We do likewise, meditating on the power of Netzach. An emerald green ball of light spins out, enveloping our body in a green bubble.

The green bubble of light lifts us up out of the Temple of

Malkuth and sets us down before the gates of Netzach.

We find ourselves standing in a rose garden with a small rose--covered temple shaped like a Georgian folly, built in the fashionable classical style. The domed roof is covered with red Roman tiles. Seven pillars made of green marble shot through with blue and red veins support the roof. White doves fly around the roof. The door is made of polished copper. In the centre of the door is an emerald set into a silver star. We say the words of power and place our palms on the copper: 'Jehovah Tzabaoth'.

The door swings inward, allowing us to enter the inner sanctum of the temple.

The first thing we notice is the beautiful smell of rose incense. In the centre is a classical altar with its sacred flame burning on the top. Above us in the middle of the domed roof is a smoke hole. Painted around the smoke hole is a seven-pointed star with a lamp suspended from each point. The floor decoration mirrors the ceiling, except that at each point of the seven-pointed star set into the floor is a colourful mosaic of one of the seven classical planets. In the centre of the star stands the altar.

As we look into the flame, it grows into the Archangel Haniel, the female angel of Netzach, called the Princess of Love and Harmony. Her swan white wings are neatly folded on her back. Her gown is the finest green silk. Her hair is like burnished copper and hangs over her shoulder. On her head is a circlet of red roses. She blesses us, and in return we ask her to show us the way to the path of Kaph.

She points behind her, and two tarot cards reveal themselves: Death and The Wheel of Fortune. It is the tarot card on the right that we need in order to step on the 21ˢᵗ path. The card itself represents the Wheel of Life. Its esoteric title is 'the Lord of the Forces of Life'.

The card shows a large wheel supported by a stone pillar. The spokes of the wheel have been decorated with a blaze of flowers and supporting greenery. Sitting on top of the wheel is the Goddess Fortuna. On her lap is the cornucopia, the fabled horn of plenty. Fruit and grain pour forth from the horn to flow down the right hand side of the Wheel of Fortune. A hound is situated likewise on the right of the wheel. On the left of the Wheel of Fortune a man ascends up the wheel. On his head is a pair of asses ears. Under the wheel lurks the serpent of knowledge.

We meditate a few moments on the scene before stepping into the card.

We find ourselves on a country path. The season is spring! The banks and verges are spotted with primroses. Bluebells hide under the shade of the trees heavy with pink and white blossom. We are young and full of the joy of life.

A troupe of Morris dancers dance up the lane in front of us, dressed in white trousers and blouses with bells strapped to their ankles. Straw hats adorned with flowers crown their heads. They jump and skip waving their handkerchiefs in the air to drive off evil spirits. We follow them onto the village green where lots of colourful folk gather around a large wooden wheel. A pretty young girl sits on the top. She has the honour to be this year's May Queen. The wheel is decorated with hawthorn blossoms and green rushes from the local brook. Everybody holds hands and starts to dance around the spring wheel.

Sitting in a bower of greenery in front of the great wheel is the Goddess Fortuna. Suspended on a gold chain around her neck hangs the Hebrew letter Kaph, symbol of the closed hand, which relates to all things kept closed and secret.

She leans forward and touches our hand with the golden Kaph, causing the hand to close into a tight fist. She then gently takes the closed fist and opens our fingers one by one, then smoothes out our palm.

Fortuna reads the lines of fate written on our palm. Once she has finished, she closes our fingers once more. What she reveals is for us alone, and guided by the symbol of the closed fist, we say nothing to anyone.

There is one thing money can't buy: that's poverty.

Someone grabs our hands and we find ourselves dancing the circle dance with the villagers. The dance has a strange timeless feel to it and, as we return to the front of the wheel again, we find that all has changed. The Wheel of Fortune has rotated a full turn and now summer holds sway; the wheel is festooned with summer flowers, along with corn sheaves and barley tops.

The May Queen is gone, replaced by a lusty male farmworker holding a frothing mug of ale. The local brass band arrive, playing in John Barleycorn, a man made of bread, with corn and barley for his hair, beard, and fingers. The figure represents the spirit of the corn field. He embodies the sacrifice of nature to bring us bread from the fields and beer from the vats.

John Barleycorn is pushed by the villagers on a handcart, then set before the great wheel. From young to old they all want a piece of John Barleycorn to insure their own good fortune and fertility. They set about eating him until there in only crumbs left.

An old man dressed as a Morris man says to us: "Don't be sad. Some of us are not destined to reach the end of our journey, but I know that come next harvest John Barleycorn will return again.

And we will hold hands and dance."

We all hold hands again and off we go in another merry round. The Wheel of Fortune turns again and heralds in autumn. The wheel is decorated with autumn leaves in rich gold and red hues.

Baskets of fruit are placed before the wheel, apples, pears, and grapes from the vine. Berries from the hedgerow lie in colourful ceramic bowls. Village children black their fingers with plump blackberries.

The villagers help themselves to the surplus bounty. Sitting like a king on top of the wheel is Bacchus, acting as master of ceremonies, festooned with grapes and crowned with vine leaves. He holds up his glass in a happy, benevolent gesture.

In the final circle dance the snow starts to fall, and the sky is grey. The Wheel turns to bring in the winter season. The wheel is decked out in bright berries, ivy, and holly, the tree of kings. Village folk let off fireworks to brighten the season and chase off bad spirits. Pumpkin lanterns glowing orange litter the village green. This is the time of refection and joy of the holiday to come when the Yule log is burnt. On top of the wheel sits the God of Misrule, looking very like Father Christmas, smiling as he waves to the crowd.

Across the green, the manor house is lit up by strings of Christmas lights. A candle burns in every window.

We are drawn to its front door by the sound of carol singing drifting across the grass. The manor house seems to shimmer with a blue haze as we approach the front door. The stout front door is made of bronze and flanked with two pillars. To enter the Temple of Chesed, we can utter the word of power: 'El'.

Since at this time we don't wish to enter the Temple of Chesed, we return to Malkuth using the name of power 'Adonai ha-Aretz'.

Visualise the temple forming around you.

The floor is made from black and white tiles. Ten black pillars shot through with gold stand around us and on the double cubic altar the sacred fame burns brightly.

Breathe in deeply and let the Temple of Malkuth gently fade.

10. 20ᵗʰ pathworking: Tiphareth to Chesed

This path, like all the paths on the Tree of Life, is made up from many different points of view.

In the tarot trump The Hermit, is the figure of the Hermit one of the Masters? That Dion Fortune alludes to in her book Mystical Qabalah, in which she assigns the Masters to the fourth Sephira, Chesed. The Masters in the Western Magical Tradition are said to be past initiates that have evolved to godlike status, having reached a level of spiritual development that puts them beyond the need to be reborn into the realm of Malkuth the Kingdom, the Earth, but join the legions of the Blessed Ones.

However, the ones called the Masters decide to return to Earth and help worthy initiates to reach their goal of spiritual union with their Holy Guardian Angel, or union with their particular God or Goddess or both.

Israel Regardie disagrees with the concept of the Masters, arguing that they are a spin off from the early obsession with spiritual mediums having spirit guides usually manifesting as American Native Indian chiefs or ancient Egyptian priests etc. returning to this earthy plane to guide and instruct.

I personally have not experienced the Masters on my magical journey, but the Hermit would make a perfect example of this phenomenon.

Most of us lesser mortals have a long way to go before we attain a place amongst the Brilliant Ones. Besides, I for one am happy to go on learning the lesson that life on planet Earth provides, and all it has to offer.

The astrological sign of the path is the constellation of Virgo. It is placed towards the end of the path as a vessel to receive the energy of the Yod (tar fire of the Gods) contained in the sacred lamp (Yoni).

Virgo is the archetypical virgin Earth Goddess. Virgo has a lot in common with the tarot card The Empress, located on the 14th path. Both hold within them the potential to re-fertilise the land if it becomes barren. Similarly, The Hermit is also a virgin. I'm not implying that virgin status is a holier than thou requirement. It implies innocents, and like the Fool, it drives us to do reckless deeds, like climbing up sacred mountains in the dark, thereby throwing yourself in the lap of the Gods!

Before we move on to the pathworking, I would like to share an anecdote from the past.

I was brought up in a little Cotswold town called Dursley, which was surrounded by wooded slopes and dominated by a conical hill called Cam Peak. Nestling under the shadow of the hill was Snake Pottery, which poured out sweet wood smoke from its outdoor wood burning kilns. Snake Pottery was housed in a small cottage with a large garden, and was also home to the Brown family. A huge totem pole decorated in the fetish style with iron nails stood outside the front of the cottage. Although frowned on by the great and the good, it drew hippies like moths to a flame. The potter's name was Pete Brown, a big man with a big beard and a big heart, Dursley's answer to Tom Bombadil.

Pete Brown fashioned large earthenware pots, jugs, and mugs with distinctive bearded faces sculptured on the front, usually in black or dark brown glazes. Frogs and newts sometimes sat inside to amaze the unwary.

Each year at Winter Solstice Pete the Potter did something remarkable. He lit a large brazier that was attached to a long pole and along with a motley crew of followers would lead them in procession up the side of Cam Peak and plant the beacon on the summit of the hill. Poems were read and mulled wine was drank and songs were sang. This took place in the 1970s, and I was one of his followers.

Pete Brown had strong feelings about money being spent on nuclear defence, and to make a political point refused to pay all his taxes, keeping back the percentage he calculated was spent on weapons of mass destruction. In answer to his refusal to pay, they sent in the bailiffs to seize his pots, which he sold from a small display in his front room.

Although friends contacted the firm of bailiffs and bought them back, his continual battle with the taxman sadly ended with a spell in prison. This led to the breakup of the family and the end of the Snake Pottery. We could do little to help at the time, but decided to keep the tradition on the Winter Solstice night alive by continuing to take fire to the hill.

Little did I know then that together with my wife Janet we would continue to take fire up the hill with our own band of followers. After the ritual, we would return to our house in Dursley to party into the wee small hours. This continued for over thirty years, until we sold our house and moved onto a narrowboat.

However, the tradition of taking fire to the hill on the Winter Solstice night lives on. Local pagans from the Gloucester area took up the mantle and now take their own flaming torch up Robinwood Hill.

So, like the Hermit leading seekers of the truth up a craggy mountain following the light from his lantern, Pete Brown started a local tradition that could go on far into the future.

If you have a convenient local hill, become the Hermit and take fire to the hill as an example to others that the light guides and enlightens.

So, it seems we were playing out the pageant of the tarot card The Hermit for years and did not realise it!

10. 20th pathworking: Tiphareth to Chesed

This is an entry from my magic diary.
Winter Solstice 20/12/99

Tonight we take fire to the hill. It's snowing outside, first time in many a year. I trust my car can make it up to the base of the hill.

After the torch is lit we process slowly up the side of Cam Peak. Once at the top I will ask the Watch Towers to say a few words, then finish with this new verse:

"We bring fire to the hill once more, on this your holy night, before the dark tide is at its full. Unlock the key to the yule tide celebrations. We ask this boon that all creatures of good heart be blessed as we ourselves are blessed. Don't question why we are here, the fact that we are here is wonder enough. Power to the sun child of the new millennium, the god and goddess and ourselves. So mote it be".

Introduction

Tiphareth to Chesed

Hebrew letter: Yod, meaning Fist or Hand
Astrological sign: Virgo
Tarot card: The Hermit
Esoteric title: Prophet of the Eternal, the Magus of the Voice of Power

Yod   20 path

The Hebrew letter Yod

The Hermit

Before we can start our adventure on the 20th path we need to rise up the Tree from our starting point in Malkuth. To this end we will invoke the Temple of Malkuth.

Create for yourself a ritual space so you feel safe and secure. When you are comfortable, balance yourself up with the Cabalistic Cross exercise.

20th pathworking

Visualise the Temple of Malkuth.

We are standing on a round raised dais. Around us are ten black marble pillars shot through with gold. The floor of the temple is constructed from black and white flagstones similar to a chessboard. In the centre is a double cubic altar upon which sits a brass lamp. Its flame rises like a pencil of light from its centre. As we look up, the pillars soar high above, their top lost in a violet mist. Gazing into the sacred flame on the altar we offer up a prayer to the Archangel Sandalphon

In answer to our prayers, the flame elongates into the form of Sandalphon.

She stands before us her snow-white wings folded on her back. Her robes of citrine, olive, russet, and black hang sensually around her flawless figure.

We ask Sandalphon for her blessing and can she help us to rise on the Tree to gain the path of Yod, the 20th path.

Sandalphon answers: "To reach your goal, follow Tiphareth, your guide."

With this advice Sandalphon lowers her slender hand over her Tiphareth centre, her heart centre. We do likewise and meditate on the power of Tiphareth. A golden ball of energy spins out enveloping our body in a golden bubble.

Our feet leave the checked floor as we rise up past the ten pillars into a golden mist. Our psychic elevator sets us down on a misty hill top. As the last of the golden mist clears, we find ourselves standing on the top of the world.

It's as if we stand at the gates of Olympus itself. Below us is the world split into four quarters like the disc of Malkuth. To the east, wind-blown mountain and high places full of beauty. Remarkable birds soar in the azure blue firmament.

Looking to the south, we see the lands of deserts and wild places where the golden lion struts, golden topped pyramids glinting in the fierce heat of the Sun. Caravans of camels cross the wasteland bringing their exotic goods to cities of the Earth.

To the west, immense oceans circle the Earth and great sailing ships plough the waves.

To the north, we see vast forests stretching their fingers out to-

wards the snows of the north, sparkling in the light of the aurora borealis.

Two herms of Apollo and Daphne guard the way. Between them is suspended a cloth of spun gold. Speaking the words of power: 'Eloah ve Daath', we breathe on the surface of the veil. The cloth of gold shimmers and is lifted by a light breeze, allowing us to pass into the inner sanctum of the Temple of Tiphareth.

The structure sits on a large well-tended lawn which is dotted all over with bright daisies. Six golden pillars shot through with purple stand on a round raised dais of white marble, their tops joined together by curved lintels coloured to match the columns. We climb up the three steps and walk into the Temple of Tiphareth. In the centre is a waist high pyramid with the top missing (truncated pyramid.)

An ornate golden bowl embellished by two cherub-shaped handles stands on the flat top of the pyramid. The solar flame rises from the centre of the bowl like a pencil of pure golden light. Surrounding the altar is a mosaic of green laurel leaves which is set into the white floor of the dais.

We offer up a prayer of blessing and thanks for arriving safely. In answers to our prayers, the flame on the altar rises up to form the figure of the Archangel Raphael, Prince of Brightness, Beauty, and Life.

Raphael rises his hand and blesses us. Turning, he points to three tapestries showing the tarot cards Justice, The High Priestess and The Hermit. It's the one on the right we want: The Hermit. As we stand in front of the tarot card The Hermit, the Hermit raises his sacred lamp above his head and moves quickly away from us. Walking into the card we hurry to catch up. We find ourselves in the foothills of barren, inhospitable mountains.

You are never too old to be young.

A stony path leads up into the mountain. We can see our guide some way up ahead, his lantern shining as a beacon. We are not alone in the mountain pass. High above us, an ancient monastery clings to its lofty perch, the Sun catching its golden roof before it sets between two distant mountain peaks.

We pass a cairn of stones supporting a pole onto which dozens of prayer flags flutter in the wind. The breeze sets free the prayers to heal the world.

Darkness falls quickly in the mountains once the Sun goes down, but we can still see the dancing light of the lantern moving up the pass before us. We notice that the light has stopped bobbing and appears to be stationary.

The going is increasingly difficult due to the failing light, so we move carefully, keeping away from the right side of the path that skirts the chasm, which drops down into the abyss. Reaching the sacred lamp, we find it abandoned on top of a large, square boulder. There is no sign of the Hermit.

In the gathering twilight, strangely coloured fluorescent lights are attracted to the lamplight like moths to a flame. These spectre-like beings dance and circle the lamp, ducking in and out of the shadows cast by the lamplight. They start to moan to the wind cries of warnings and omens.

"You're not worthy to carry the lamp of the sacred Yod! It is the holy seed of creation," they moan.

"Return to the golden Temple of Tiphareth before you become imprisoned inside the lamp like the genies of old, to wander through time carried by a holy fool!

"The light of faith is the ultimate burden, leave it be, go now!"

The moaning, taunting voices make our head spin. We place our hands over our ears to block them out. Trying to think logically, we ask ourselves: "What exactly is a lamp for?"

The answer comes to us in a flash: "It shows us the way in the darkness."

If we return down the mountain in the dark, we are more than likely to fall off the track into oblivion. However, if we retrace our steps back down the pass the same fate probably awaits you. So, without further thought we pick up the sacred lamp flooding the path before us with its sacred light.

The way down is clear to us now, and the genies of the seven lamps vanish into the surrounding darkness. We are alone under the starry vault of heaven that crowns the lofty mountain tops.

Holding the lamp before us, we descend down the steep path. The way is considerably easier traveling downhill, nevertheless we still stumble now and then.

A ragged shrub grows at the side of the path. We stop to investigate; a simple wooden staff has been left in its branches for us to retrieve. Staff in one hand, lamp in the other, we safely descend down the mountain pass.

The path ahead starts to become lighter as the Moon clears the horizon. The path levels out and we discover a small clearing surrounded by sparse bushes, inside which is one of the ancient thrones of coronation. Sat on the throne and bathed in moonlight is Virgo, the virgin queen of the Earth.

She looks us in the eyes and says; "Welcome to my bower. I am the virgin queen of the Earth. You carry inside your lamp the sacred Yod, God's fire, the sacred sperm of life, and in your hand, you carry the staff of life, the phallus of regeneration! It's time to pass them on," says the virgin queen, holding out her hands. Gently we pass the lantern to Virgo. She smiles and opening the glass front she takes out the shinning Yod and absorbs it into her belly, where it glows within. Instinctively we pass her the staff, which she pushes into the hard ground with no effort, and the earth swallows up the end like a lover.

Like the holy thorn of Glastonbury, the staff takes root and bursts into growth, leaves sprouting as life is renewed. All life seems to flow from the Goddess that sits before us. The path we have been following springs into life. Vines, flowers, and all earthly delights of Mother Nature stretch out before us. We find ourselves walking down out of the mountain pass into a fertile valley that leads to the Temple of Chesed. It's like arriving at the Emerald City, only it's blue, not green. Chesed stands before us, a perfect example of the city state. This could be Atlantis or maybe Troy: 'the golden age of man' created the city state as a haven against the harsh world they were born into. Chesed represents the peak of architecture, art, and learning, however brief.

The rain falls on the just and unjust alike.

The doors are massive and art deco in style. Twin antelopes spring across the polished bronze surface. Lifting the heavy bronze knocker which is shaped like a dove, we let it drop and intone the words of power: 'El'.

The sound of the knocker booms out and the doors slowly swing inwards.

The pattern of the temple is similar to the others, except the dais is square and reached by four steps. Four pillars, strong blue shot through with black jet, stand at each corner. The floor of the Temple of Chesed is made of light green tiles. The altar is a pyramid, a perfect tetrahedron, its four sides equal and complete in their symmetry. Their four points meet as one at the apex. The sapphire capstone receives the energy that flows down from above, bringing the holy power of Binah the great sea into the centre of the temple. In so doing, the four sides of the pyramid emit the archetypal idea of the four elements expressed fully in the Kingdom of Malkuth.

Blue flames flicker from the top of the pyramid. We fancy we can see dancing figures. Perhaps it's the Chasmalim, the Brilliant ones, the order of angels of Chesed.

Meditating on the flame we offer up a prayer to Tzadkiel, Archangel of Chesed.

The flame grows until it takes on the form of Tzadkiel.

Tzadkiel is Jovian in appearance and wears a toga in the Roman style. His wings are white, tinged with blue. He has a full beard and holds a golden lyre on which he plays the music of the spheres (wow! At last an angel with a harp!)

"The ancients believed that you could hear the music generated by the motion of planets, called the music of the spheres."

When we are ready to return to Malkuth, we thank the Archangel Tzadkiel, utter the words of power 'Adonai ha-Aretz' and visualise the Temple of Malkuth once more.

Its floor is made up from black and white tiles. Ten columns of black marble shot through with gold dwarf us. In the centre stands the double cubic altar which supports the sacred flame.

Take a deep breath and let the temple fade.

122

11. 19th pathworking: Geburah to Chesed

Strength (Fortitude) or La Forza.

The image on the tarot card Strength is usually a young woman wearing a hat or with a cosmic lemniscate over her head (a figure--of-eight ribbon, symbol of eternity.)

She is shown subduing a lion with little effort on her part. In some of the early packs Strength portrays by Hercules slaying the Nemean Lion.

For the purpose of this pathworking it is best to use image of a woman subduing a lion. Who is this brave young woman? The origin of the figure is thought to be Cyrene, a hand maiden of the hunter Moon Goddess Artemis.

The legend tells that one day the Sun looked down from his fiery chariot and spotted a young nymph, Cyrene, wrestling a large male lion barehanded, holding his mouth open with apparent ease. Her triumphant air of beauty won the heart of the Sun. After obtaining sound advice on how to proceed from Chiron, the wisest of Centaurs (after all, she was one of Artemis' hand maidens and obviously one tough cookie!) he managed to carry her off in his chariot. There was a child of this union, a son called Aristaeus the huntsman god. One of his gifts was power over animals.

Ancient occultists believed that certain people also possessed magical powers over the animal kingdom. To help win domination over animals, it is said that a talisman using the iconography of a young woman (Fortitude) subduing a lion, would endow you with the necessary gift to help control unruly animals. So, slip your tarot card Strength into your pocket and you will turn into a right little Dr Doolittle.

The image of the lion and the unicorn incorporated into British royal coat of arms has similar properties to the tarot card Strength. The lion is the symbol of the Sun and the unicorn is the symbol of the Moon and virginity, purity over sexual vigour. Similar images of a graceful unicorn resting his noble head on the lap of a virgin maid is the stuff of pre-Raphaelite ardour.

In the following pathworking, in the temple of earthly delights, two subdued lions flanking Fortuna are an example of this phenomenon in action.

On the tarot card Strength, the symbology also points to the mastery of the five senses, hearing, sight, taste, smell, and touch. Don't forget that elusive sixth sense, the ability to probe the astral field around you, and those things that hide beyond the veil. The universe reveals itself through your senses and when all six are employed to their full potential the sensual range is awesome. The colours on your TV set are all made up of just three colours and see what a kaleidoscope of colours they create.

The point I'm trying to make is, don't take your sensual gifts for granted. The warm moist kiss when lovers embrace, the smell of perfumed smoke traveling on a desert wind, sweet music to move your soul and quicken your heart beat – sheer heaven!

Introduction
Geburah to Chesed

Hebrew letter: Teth, meaning Snake
Astrological sign: Leo
Tarot card: Strength
Esoteric title: the Daughter of the Flaming Sword

Hebrew letter Teth

Strength.

Before we can start our adventure on the 19th path, we need to rise up the Tree from Malkuth. To this end we will invoke the Temple of Malkuth.

Create for yourself a ritual space so you feel safe and secure. When you are comfortable, balance yourself and cleanse your aura with the Cabalistic Cross exercise.

125

19th pathworking

Visualise the Temple of Malkuth.

We are standing on a round raised dais. Around us are ten black marble classic pillars shot through with gold. The floor of the temple is constructed from black and white flagstones like a chessboard. In the centre is a double cubic altar upon which sits an open lamp. Its flame rises tall and bright from its centre. As we look up, the pillars soar high above us their tops lost in a violet mist. Gazing into the flame on the altar we offer up a prayer to the Archangel Sandalphon.

In answer to our prayers, the flame elongates into the form of Sandalphon.

She stands before us, her snow-white wings folded on her back. Her robes of citrine, olive, russet, and black hang sensually around her perfect body.

We ask Sandalphon for her blessing and if she can help us to rise on the Tree to gain the 19 the path, the path of the Hebrew letter Teth.

Sandalphon answers: "To reach your goal, follow Geburah, your guide."

With this advice, Sandalphon lowers her slender hand over her right shoulder. We do likewise, meditating on the power of Geburah. A ball of red energy spins out, enveloping our body in a red bubble.

Our feet leave the checked floor as we rise up past the ten pillars into the red mist. Our psychic elevator sets us down before iron doors set into the marble plinth that glow with concealed power.

The surface of the gates is decorated with heroic figures similar to the images you would see on a Greek urn. To enter the temple of Geburah, we place our hands on the iron doors and intone the words: 'Elohim Gibor'.

The iron doors swing silently inwards. The Temple of Geburah is built on a raised dais. The floor of the temple is constructed from brick red mosaic, into which has been worked a huge pentagram of green jade tesserae.

Fire-red pillars shot through with iron stand between the points of the pentagram. In the centre of the pentagram is the pentagon formed by the lines of the inner pentagram. Here stands the altar. It is a strange device: two bronze hunting dogs sitting up back to back. A simple hammered iron bowl sits firmly on their four ears. From the iron bowl rises the Martial flame. It rises up like a pencil of red neon light.

Above our head is the starry vault of heaven, swimming in an ocean of indigo eternity. That is Binah.

We offer up a prayer to the Archangel Khamael: Prince of Strength and Courage. As we gaze into the flame on the altar the ruby flame elongates into the figure of the Archangel Khamael. Khamael is dressed like a Roman or Greek warrior. He is young in appearance, but ageless. His wing are small and dove-like, with a red tinge. On his breast plate is the image of Medusa.

We ask him to open the way onto the 19th pathworking for us.

Khamael blesses us and points behind the altar. Two tapestries appear. The one on the left shows the tarot card The Chariot, the tapestry on the right reveals Strength. It is Strength we need to walk the 19th path.

The tapestry shows a young woman subduing a lion. The tarot card draws us in and we find ourselves standing in a gladiatorial arena, similar to a bull fighting ring. Young warriors, both men and women, circle each other in a meditative dance. They are armed with spears and swords.

"They risk the greatest thing they possess: their own bodies."

Turning around to see who spoke we come face to face with

Archangel Khamael dressed like a Greek hero, his red-tinged wings transparent and misty.

Khamael speaks again: "True warriors right wrongs and restore universal balance in the name of the Red Ray and the Sephira Geburah. Intellectuals tend to despise violence, but their citadels of learning would fall like ripe fruit into the hands of the ignorant and cruel if it was not for the warrior class. So, find in yourself the true ruby light of Geburah, to give you pride and strength in times when words are not heeded without the sight of the naked sword."

We thank Khamael for his words of wisdom. We might not feel like warriors, but to walk tall we need to be able to conjure the Red Ray in times of peril.

Khamael puts his finger to his lips in the sign of silence. We perform the same action. Now we can observe without being seen or heard. Khamael leads us through the fighters to the tunnel at the other side of the stadium that leads out into the street. Khamael sees us safely into the tunnel, then with a final word of farewell returns to the training ground.

The area behind the stadium is full of market stalls, selling all manner of spices and bright silk garments, pots and pans, all sorts of things. We seem to be in the Far East, maybe India?

Crowds of people mill about the market square. A road leads out of the market. Single storey houses line the street and sacred cows sway down the middle of the road adorned with flowers, brass bells clanging from their necks. The crowd parts to let them through. We do likewise. Bringing up the rear is a troupe of Buddhist monks in their striking saffron robes. Each carries a wooden bowl. Women in splendid saris come out of the houses and pour rice and pieces of fruit into their begging bowls. They pay us little heed as they pass us by.

We stop to watch a snake charmer who sits cross-legged on

the side of the street. From a large basket, the hood of a cobra emerges. He moves back and forth to the rhythm of the snake charmers' pipe. His huge body undulates out of the basket, iridescent scales twinkle in the sun-baked street. Lifting his hooded head, he stares coolly with black beady eye straight at us. As we move on quickly, he watches our process making us feel vulnerable.

When we reach what seems to be the centre of town, there is a magnificent bee-hived shaped temple. Brightly painted figures of people making love in all the positions possible and impossible cover the outside walls.

This is the temple of earthly delights, similar in style to the Hindu Sun temple of Konark in the Indian state of Odisha.

The invitation is obvious, so we enter. Inside the temple the air is as warm as the womb and rich with the smell of incense and perfumes. Many slim pastel-coloured pillars support the domed ceiling. In the shadows hooded lamps of many colours feed the hidden places with seductive low light.

It is so erotic you can taste it. The centre of the temple is the epicentre of the 19th path. There on a raised dais sitting in the lotus position is Strength. Two lions crouch on each side of her with their heads on their paws.

In her lap is a beaten brass tray on which sits the golden Hebrew letter Teth. Strength looks deep into our soul beseeching us to come forward. When we stand before the strange apparition of Strength, she offers up the tray to us. We place our hand gently on the symbol of Teth. The Yod at its head glows with golden fire and is transformed for a moment into a snake's head, the symbol's tail swaying like the snake in the street. It caresses the back of our hand with a long seductive forked tongue. Strength moves the Teth and tray back onto her lap and whispers one word: 'Sit!'

We sit crossed legged before the dais and let the strange force of Teth flow through us, as Teth dances serpent-like in the flames on the tray. We feel our own inner snake stir deep in the heart of our Yesod centre. This is Kundalini, the serpent that sleeps at the base of our spine.

Feel the warmth of the Odic force filling your lower triangle from your Yesod, sexual zone, up to the top of your hips, where sit the Sephiroth of Hod and Netzach.

Once full, the golden snake of Kundalini rises up through the lower triangle reaching for the sacred heart centre of Tiphareth. If you feel comfortable, let your sexual energy embrace the spiritual.

As the Kundalini snake coils around the Akashic egg at the heart of Tiphareth, the union is complete. The silver of the Moon centre joins with the Sun at the heart centre.

Somewhere deep in the temple of earthly delights a gong sounds. Its deep vibration calls us back to the path. The Kundalini snake returns to our Yesodic centre to coil up and sleep once more, like a genie in a bottle just waiting to be summoned again.

Your biggest erogenous zone is your brain.

We shake off our euphoria, and standing up, bow to the Lady Strength and her twin lions. We turn and make our way through the temple to the exit, back onto the street.

As we walk down the street, we feel invigorated by our union with our inner Tiphareth. Unperturbed, we walk out past the last buildings that straddle the edge of the town, making our way down a country road. Green fields flank the road in this semi-farmed paradise. Little paths lead off to the odd farm buildings. In the dis-

tance stands a mountain range. Dark storm clouds suddenly gather before us, obscuring the mountains. They close in on us quickly, as the storm marches across the tops of lush trees. The rain comes down in a tropical downpour. The rain is warm and refreshing, reminding us strangely of the temple of earthly delights! Distant thunder rolls across the heavens, and lightning snakes through the rain turning it into golden arrows of light.

We stand there, our arms outstretched to receive the blessing of Jupiter lord of Olympus and king of Gods, who is reputed to appear sometimes in a shower of golden rain.

The golden rain parts before us like a curtain and there standing before us is the Temple of Chesed.

If you wish to enter the Temple of Chesed, place the palm of your hands on the polished bronze doors and intone the name of power 'El' and the doors with swing inward. If, however, you wish to return to the Temple of Malkuth vibrate the words of power: 'Adonai ha-Aretz' and visualise the Temple of Malkuth once more.

The floor is made up of black and white tiles. Ten black pillars shot through with gold stand around us. The eternal flame burns on the double cubic altar.

With a deep breath let the temple slowly fade, and return to your normal state of consciousness.

Afterword

Once you have travelled the lateral 19th path between Geburah and Chesed, this concludes the last of the eight paths that make up the Witches' Hexagram. I earnestly trust you will travel the paths often until you have built up your own special bond with the inner planes. Working with the paths and Sephiroth is similar to reading an adventure novel. You can experience the high seas in Treasure Island, and enjoy the villainous machinations of the loveable rogue Long John Silver in his obsession with buried treasurer, or be sucked into the world of Lord of the Rings which most certainly has changed many people's outlook on life.

The experiences and lessons learnt working with the Tree of Life in the Western Magical Tradition will not only enrich your mind, but for some may enrich your soul. Similar to a novel, the world of the Cabalah is accessible from your own fireside chair through the medium of Hermetic practises, with the addition of modern Wiccan rituals and processes, and a large spoonful of dedicated study. Learn all the symbols that the tarot has to offer and the Hebrew letters that make their home on the graph of the Tree of Life.

The right addition of the physical applications of incense, perfume, music and light will enhance your Cabalistic knowledge to new heights.

The reward for all this hard work is respect from your fellow practitioners, and you will be seen not just as another Witch but as a Witch and Magician.

Above all have fun, be safe and guard your loved ones.

Always strive to be perfect, and one day you can say: "I myself was once touched by genius."

Bibliography

Dear Reader, if you can find room on your bookshelf for a few more books, I have listed a short bibliography that I have found interesting and inspiring.

Crowley Vivianne, *Wicca, A Comprehensive Guild to the old Religion in the Modern World*, Harper Collins Publishers

Hutton Ronald, *Triumph of the Moon*, Oxford University Press

Hutton Ronald, *Witch*, Oxford University Press

McCormack Kathleen, *Tarot*, Fontana Books

Gayley Charles Mills, *Classic Myths in English Literature*, Gim and Company

Crowley Aleister, *The Book of Thoth*, Samuel Weiser Inc.

Wang Robert, *The Qabalistic Tarot*, Samuel Weiser Inc.

Shakespeare William, *A Midsummer Night's Dream*, Methuen & Co.

Knight Gareth, *A Practical Guide to Qabalistic Symbolism*, vol. 1 and 2, Helios

Fortune Dion, *Moon Magic*, The Aquarian Press

Fortune Dion, *Sea Priestess*, The Aquarian Press

Sturzaker James, *Kabbalistic Aphorisms*, Metatron Press

Williams Jean and Cox Zachary, *The Gods Within*, Moondust Book

Bibliotheca Alexandrina

We are a Pagan and occult publishing house established by two witches, Enenna and Velkan, who share love for books and the Alexandrian tradition. We started out with bringing such classic authors as Doreen Valiente, Starhawk and Vivianne Crowley to the Polish audience.

Robert Hardy's "The Witches' Pyramid" and "The Witches' Hexagram" are our first two original works published in English, and the first two of planned three works with Cabbalistic pathworkings.

www.bibliotheca-alexandrina.co.uk